Ekaterina's Journey

To the Bullocks
дякаю мега!

Lidiya Herrington
2014! x

Ekaterina's Journey

From the Donbass to Darfield

A Biography

Translated and Written by Lidiya Herrington

Editing by Vee O'Brien

Although I have tried to remain faithful to what Mama said. At a distance of over half a century some memories are understandably incomplete, and where necessary I have used our own research, imaginations and knowledge to fill in the gaps.

However, the essence of the stories related here are true as they were told by Mama who experienced them at first hand. With regard to the early history Mama's Mum and Grandma told her the history of the family.

© Lidiya Herrington, 2012

Illustrations copyright © 2012 Lidiya Herrington/Jack Etherington

Published by Lidiya Herrington 2014 for the Cieslik Family 2014

A CIP catalogue record for this book is available from the British Library.

ISBN 978-0-9928303-0-4

Book layout and design by Clare Brayshaw

Prepared and printed by:

York Publishing Services Ltd
64 Hallfield Road
Layerthorpe
York YO31 7ZQ

Tel: 01904 431213

Website: www.yps-publishing.co.uk

Contents

Acknowledgements

In translating my Mother's tapes it led me down a path that I really didn't want to go. But as I started to listen to that familiar voice, that had been a constant safety net all my life, it gave me a purpose. To leave her legacy, so that future generations will know from where their first roots were laid in Britain.

I would like to thank my husband Terry for all his help and support during the writing of this book. My sister Vee and her husband Dave. Vee for all the months of travelling up and down the motorway, through sun, rain and snow to type and edit the book so magnificently. (All this for a bowl of soup.)

Tony and Carol McNicholas for their advice, even though Tony tried to escape before I could ask for his opinion. (He usually failed).

My sister Val and brother David, always willing to listen to snippets I had translated, my brother Michael and all my friends.

I hope that you and all our families feel the pride and awe of what our parents lived through, and I wish that my other sister Anna could have lived to read it, but I'm sure that her daughters will get comfort from her history.

All my love and gratitude.

Lidiya

Babooshka drawn by grandson Antony

Foreword

On a hot summer's day in the middle of July an elderly lady lovingly tendered her garden. Her daughter had bought her a new camellia which she had to water in the heat.

A sharp pain in her stomach made her stop abruptly. It had occurred before but this time it was more severe. She made her way back to the house and told her friend Ernest of her problem. He was concerned so decided to take her to the hospital in his car and within a short time she was in Barnsley Hospital. Michael her son was staying with her at the time so Ernest informed him of the problem with his mother.

Michael called his sister Lidiya and her husband as they lived close to the hospital and they rushed to her side. Michael joined them a little time later. Arriving at the ward they could see Mama was in great pain. " Ya Tut Mama, Ya Tut Mama" Lidiya said in Ukrainian. "I am here Mama, I am here."

The consultant said that tests had to be made but it looked like a bowel had burst and that she would need an emergency operation. If that was the case then due to her age it was possible that she only had a 5% chance of surviving it, but if the operation didn't take place then she would certainly die anyway.

"I want my family" she said. We've already informed them and they're on their way. "They're coming Mama, we love you" Lidiya replied. During the agonising hours that followed all the family arrived throughout the morning with the exception of Ann who lived in Canada and was in the process of looking for a flight home. The porters came to take her down to the theatre. She looked up and said "I won't be back." Putting her hands together she repeated "I won't be back, but I'm happy. I'm going to a better place." As they wheeled her away, we kissed her, she looked back and said "I'm not leaving you, tell my family I love them and look after Nicky."

After what seemed like an eternity a doctor ushered the family into a small room to tell them the outcome of the operation. "Well!" he said, "that is one very tough lady in there. She survived the operation but the next few days will be crucial. She is in the Intensive Care Unit so we will do our very best to keep her alive." At least we had some hope, but in our hearts we knew it would be a miracle if she lived.

During the next couple of weeks the family took it in turns to keep a vigil by her bed. It seemed at times as if we had some hope but the doctors needed to move her into a private room on a ward and it only seemed a matter of time before the inevitable happened.

On August 4th 2006 surrounded by most of her children and grandchildren Katya died as Russian/Ukrainian music played on a small cassette and her daughter Lidiya stroked her and her daughter Vee stroked her face. "Mama" Lidiya said in Ukrainian. "Go to your beloved sunflower fields. Go to your Mama." All her children, grandchildren, daughters-in-law and sons-in-law went to kiss her. She gave a sigh and peacefully passed away.

A funeral was held in the ancient church in Darfield. She was carried to the church in a white glass sided coach pulled by two white horses. Her coffin was carried by her grandsons and she was finally buried in the grave of her husband Michael in a peaceful area of the churchyard.

During the 2 weeks that followed her house in Maran Avenue had to be cleared of her precious possessions. One by one they were shared between her children and grandchildren. Under her bed there were many documents all written in Ukrainian. Previously there had been several cassette tapes recorded by her in Ukrainian and English and given to all her children.

Her daughter Lidiya decided to translate her tapes and record them as a book and record of the family history. What unfolded was a fantastic account of her Mother's early life, just after the Russian revolution and the invasion by the Germans and her subsequent capture.

Chapter One

1870-1914

Now I'm going to tell of the lives and history of my grandparents and great grandparents. I would like to think my children, grandchildren, great grandchildren and maybe others, may be interested in my life and to know the history of a Ukrainian person.

I was told the family's history as a child by my mother, grandma and other relatives as we sat on an evening.

This story began a long, long time ago.

1870 – 1914

My great grandad, my mother's grandad, was a gospodin (gentleman); they lived in the Carpathians (or somewhere near the Carpathians). The Carpathians have forests and mountains. My great grandparents lived in a village called Horochanski (Horokhiv) in the Stanislavaski regions. Now Stanislavaski is named Ivan Frankivsk region (West Ukraine).

It was built on the site of the village Zabolottya in 1662. During the period of Polish reign it was named Stanislawow later Stanislava. In 1962 Stanislava was renamed Ivan Frankivsk in honour of the famous Ukrainian writer, Slav scholar, and philosopher Ivan Franko. The Carpathian Mountains are 40 minutes drive from the city.

By my mother's stories, or maybe I heard my grandma tell, of a beautiful Ukrainian land, that lovely place, of villages and of a land that was blanketed with sunflower fields, orchards, flowers, rivers flowing, everything green.

For centuries our country, Ukraine, has been invaded by different enemies; Tartars, Hungarians, Turks, a long history of attacks on the land, Poles, Germans – everyone wanted the fertile land, the country that is maybe the best in the ex Soviet Union. Of course, I know there are other beautiful places, but for me, it is the Ukraine with its sunflowers and the golden wheat fields. As a young girl I saw the beauty of that land, on my way to water the allotments with water from the river. When anyone goes now, they see how lovely Ukraine is and places there, and the warm hearted Slavonic people.

My grandad and grandma and their parents dwelt in the Carpathian Mountains. They were from the Hutul tribe of whom I will tell you later. The forests were very beautiful. In those forests they had mushrooms, nuts, strawberries and different types of berries. In those forests there was wealth. Besides that in the forest were bears, wolves, wild boar and foxes.

Now what I want to say is that my grandad was the son of a gentleman. The gentleman was my great grandad but my great grandad's father was unknown. He was left at the gates of a priest's house. (It was thought that maybe an unmarried girl had left him). That's one history.

Now my grandma was the daughter of a forester. Rich people owned forests and some forests were large so they employed men to look after them. They had a house close to the woods and they looked after the forest. My grandad was from a gentleman's family. I don't know much, but my grandparents were married.

They say Horochanski was a wonderful place – a village with a river running through it. The houses had thatched roofs; people who were wealthier had roofs made of corrugated iron or slates. This is how the houses were built. A gate would be put up, trees planted, then the straw was mixed with the mud. This then was used to build a cottage. The mud mix was smoothed and levelled; when it was dry they painted it in whitewash. Little houses stood all white. Then of course they put on the thatch. Inside there was an oven but it was made that so when it cooled down children could sleep on it. Though people who were wealthier did not live like this. Ordinary people had some land, a cow, chickens, pigs, gardens and orchards. They baked their own bread and rambled in the forests collecting berries, mushrooms etc. There were wild animals, so I was told.

People gathered in the harvest, they sorted it and took the hay for cattle. In the woods there were wild boar, bears, foxes and wolves. A family anecdote was that one evening, a bear climbed onto the plum tree whose branches hung over the house and the bear fell into the house, because of course the roof was not strong. Foxes stole the chickens, and wolves often tried to attack, so people went out in teams for protection.

I remember a couple more anecdotes that I was told.

A gentleman/farmer said someone is stealing my grain so he went into the barn, climbed up the ladder into the loft and he sat waiting to catch the man who was stealing his grain, but no one was stealing his grain. Anyway, he lay in wait in the loft, then he heard a commotion just before dawn, what it was was a bear running in. The bear was followed by wild boar that were chasing him. The bear ran up the ladders to the loft and started to throw down the bales at the boars. The pigs got flustered, and ran off, the bear was so agitated he carried on and threw the farmer from the loft.

A story Gran told of when a "Jewish" buyer came to buy corn from them, she hid a couple of buckets of his grain, he noticed and got so angry that he scattered all the corn.

Every Sunday young girls got dressed up in their national costumes, wore their embroidered blouses, skirts, aprons and waistcoats. On their heads they wore coronets of flowers, necklaces on their chests, and lots of ribbons hanging from the flower coronets. Different regions had different costumes and different customs. Usually they went to church then to the fairs.

Now I want to tell how my grandad and grandma lived. Their surname was Dubas (Dub is oak in the Ukrainian language). My gran was small, a lovely lady. My grandad was tall, that's how I remember him, he died young about 1930/31 and he loved me very much. I was his first grandchild. It's funny what events you remember as a child. I remember him often brushing my hair looking for head lice.

Their life

They had a smallholding. They had children as I remember being told, lots of children, but a lot died; in those days you didn't have the medicines like now. There was one incident when gran went to the fields to cut the wheat. There she gave birth to a child, wrapped it up and took the child home. That's how it was in those days.

A river flowed through the village. They went to the river to do their laundry. There was a stone that was used to beat the clothes against. You had to go to the river for water. My grandad was very strict. In those days men thought women were of a lower order, he was the master and what he said, or did, it had to be so. Mostly women were afraid of husbands and fathers. There was one incident when a man beat his wife and she went to her parents' house. Her father also beat her for leaving her husband then took his daughter to her spouse, that's the sort of life my grandma had.

Grandad was a good provider but he also had some nasty sides to his nature. He once told grandma that he was going to take a mistress, who was a godmother to one of their children, and lived somewhere across the river. Of course this made my gran very nervous, naturally, because if he got another woman gran couldn't please him whatever she did. Many times she used to hide in the hay or shed as he used to beat her. People were very religious then, they were afraid of sin but somehow may I say they were strict and cruel.

Something that happened years later, I remember because I have a good memory, and I see the scene as if it is replayed on a screen. It was Holy Night (Christmas Eve), every family as the dusk approached had to have 12 dishes prepared. Every dish had to be pisnya (meatless).

Well! My grandma had many children but only 6 survived, 2 sons and 4 daughters. Vasil was the eldest, then came Mama Anya followed by Lena, Nyoosa, Fedya and Maroosya. My gran's name was Parasca and my grandad's Dimitri.

Well, in those days, people toiled very hard; they had to bring the water from the well. They had to bake, cook, graze the cows, feed the pigs, chickens, geese and ducks to be fed, see to the small children. And all this had to be done by nightfall. As dusk fell, people sat round the table, and everything must be prepared. Dishes like Kutya were made from wheat berries. There were different types of vareniki (pasta dumplings with different fillings) and this and that dish. But everything had to be without meat.

One Holy Night, grandma so tried to make it a success, she worked really hard to have everything ready for nightfall. My grandad had been to the godmother (lover) and came home drunk. Now my gran was frightened of him, but she said "Dimitri why have you come home so late, Holy Night is approaching and the meal has to be set." "What do you need" he replied. "Maybe you want me to bring some water for you?" Even if you bring some water, gran said, it would help. So he took the buckets and went some distance to the river to fetch the water.

Then what do you think he did? Because he was drunk and a drunk doesn't know what he is doing, he tipped a bucket of water over the doorstep into the room. The floor of the room was made of a clay soil that was levelled out even and smoothed. so of course it went slimy when wet. Gran started wailing, "Don't touch me." He turned around and went somewhere to sleep it off, and that was my gran's Holy Night.

One of the customs, at Christmas, was to have a tray covered with an embroidered cloth. On it was placed Kutya (a traditional Ukrainian central dish, a wheatberry and poppy seed pudding, that is served on Holy Night) and other snacks. This the children of the house took to their grandparents, godparents or relatives, and in return were given money. That's how things were then, life went on.

I know my family came from the Carpathians, gentlemen foresters, but no one was wealthy. It was said my great great grandad was a priest. He was wealthy because priests had a tendency to be wealthy. My mama told me about when she was a servant in a priest's house. He had land, where he had cows, horses pigs. Quite a number of servants. People bowed to the priests kissed their hands and feet, gave them gifts. My mama said they ate, drank, entertained guests, and had balls. Their children and their children's children had everything.

When it was Easter time, everyone gathered and went to the church all night. A cake like a sweet bread was baked; the taller it was the more it was admired. This cake is named paska (the word paska is Easter in the Slavonic language). Boiled eggs were coloured and decorated. One of the dyes was made by boiling eggs in onions skins. There was salo (salted pork fat), horseradish made into a sauce, salami and bread. These were taken to church to be blessed by the priest.

All this was after fasting for a few weeks (Lent), people arrived in Church and worshipped. All night services were conducted as choirs sang. Then just before dawn before the cockerel started singing the priest would come out sprinkling holy water on the paskhas (cakes) and other items that were brought, making the sign of the cross over them. Then everyone started to disperse home.

Some families started celebrating straight away, and other families went to sleep for a while and then started celebrating. Every family all sat round the table, which had the food that had been blessed on it, eat the paskha, painted eggs, salami, horseradish. There was holodets (brawn) that was a popular dish. Then after breakfast they went visiting family and friends or received guests. The festivities lasted a couple of days. They drank, ate and partied. That was how the festival was.

After a week, (I was told), on the following Sunday a similar thing was repeated. Everyone went to the cemetery or church burial grounds and cleared and tidied the graves. With them they took the blessed paskha and decorated boiled eggs. They gathered round their respective ancestors graves and placed some on the grave. The rest of the food was then distributed amongst the poor.

Later, maybe next day, the priest would go round on a large horse and cart to the villages, blessing the homes sprinkling holy water and making the sign of the cross. In return he was given money, some bread, some gave him eggs. Of course a lot of people didn't have money so they gave what they had. In those days they didn't really have the sense to question why the priest would want all this food.

My mama worked as a servant at the priest's house. She told me that when he got back to his estate he would give some to the workers in his employ the rest was fed to the pigs and chickens. That was the custom in those days. He wasn't to blame of course, that was part of his work, and seeing as he couldn't eat everything what else could he do. My mama said that when it was Lent the priests didn't fast, they had what they fancied.

A story my Gran told me. When the priest went to visit a man and left his horse near the grain, the man went and tethered the horse near some straw. The priest was so annoyed, when this man went to church to have his child christened the priest named him Straw.

My mama worked at the priests for a year. Then as the year came to an end, her father came to collect her wages, and then leave her to work for the master for another year. People lived in that lovely place, content with their lives. That was the only life they knew, the rhythm of life in the Carpathians.

Chapter Two

1914 – 1918

Then the war started

That war wasn't like modern warfare. My gran told me, Austro-Hungarian and German soldiers (then, that part of the Carpathian Mountains was under Austro-Hungarian rule) were dug in on one side, with the Russians on the opposite side in the trenches. They shot at one another, advanced, and then fell back. In my gran's village the Rusani (Russians) were dug in, but when evening came they got together with the Austro-Hungarians and Germans, smoked cigarettes, discussed things. Then the following day they would start fighting again.

Soldiers then, as now, can get out of hand, so the villagers had dugouts in the forests to hide their girls, so they wouldn't be raped. Gran recalled how she hid her daughters in the hay. My mama said when night fell the soldiers were on the prowl looking for girls. They were hidden deep inside the hay where gran had covered them. Then bayonets started to pierce the straw, my mama said she nearly got stabbed in the eye, but they weren't discovered. That was what it was like in that place Horochanski.

Day after day the battles continued; sounds of guns shooting. Evenings would be quiet but as daylight approached the gunfire would start again, and the noise of little cottages burning. Don't forget the cottages had straw roofs. So this war went on and on. People lived in fear, but in the end they had to step back (retreat) from their dear homeland, their little corner where they had grown up in those Carpathian Mountains and forests. Where they had spent their childhood, where their grandparents had lived, where they originated from, I don't know. Every place is dear when it is your home, and they were very sad to leave their beloved

Horohlinoo, their home to go far away to an unknown place. Like the sadness I felt when I came to England in my lifetime. (more information in the Glossary)

A great battle started. My gran had just proved some dough preparing to make bread, but this did not come to pass. Outside the Russians started to retreat. The Germans started to advance on the village so gran's family also had to start to retreat. Grandad prepared the horses, got the cow, put what they could on the cart and started their long unknown journey from their dear home to wander through foreign fields and orchards. My grandad I heard was a patriot Ukrainian, he was against the Germans, the Poles and the Austro-Hungarians. He couldn't stay in his village to be ruled by someone else so made the decision to go to Kiev. Gran said that it was a dream of his to see Kiev as he saw it as the heart of the Ukraine.

What could they do? Turmoil of war. The children were small, there were food shortages, they had to go on. Through those golden fields, through woods, across rivers, a long unknown road to travel. They didn't know what awaited them. A long, long way they walked. Not only they were tramping the road, others were in the same situation. Husbands, wives, children, old people. All the young men were at the battlefields.

On and on they walked, over the golden fields and steppes which in previous times had been ruled over by Germans, Tartars and Hungarians. Our beloved Ukraine. They walked and walked and walked. It was difficult with small children. I don't know how many months they were on the road. The cow fell down, later the horse also died, so they loaded what they could on barrows. My mama was born in 1897, so in 1914 she was 17 years of age. Others were probably 12, 10 – I really don't know, but they were younger. Gradually, as they were on their way to their destination Kiev, they came to a place between Uman and Kiev a village called Ivanko near Ivanko-Frankivsk town. Anyhow they set up camp on the outskirts of the town, in the fields, around were woods. Tents were made the best they could, with sunflower sticks or old tree branches, they were like gypsies. Then off they went, begging round the villages for bread and potatoes, and anything else that was spare. Now the rain had started, then the frost, cold. Local people helped them, started to take the refugees to their homes. These evacuees were called Avstriti – Austrian refugees. The reason they were called (Austriti) Austrian refugees was because the part of Ukraine they were from was under Austrian rule. Here they started another life. Relatives who refused to leave the old place were left there in the Carpathians. My mama told me it was difficult to ask for bread and potatoes, begging, it was so shameful.

Later an old woman gave them a house. She had 2 houses; one stood at the side of a lane, the other house was further back in the orchard where the old woman lived. There were 2 or 3 rooms, I don't know how many but there was my gran, granddad and 6 children. Not far from the house was a white clay mine. There was a clay mound, then a small bridge over the river and a lane straight down to the sugar beet factory. The left of the house led to the village centre, if you turned right you'd arrive at the woods. These woods had mushrooms, nuts, wild pear, crab apples and as in their previous life the family would go gathering mushrooms, fruits, berries, then preserve them for winter – drying and pickling the produce of their labour, especially mushrooms were dried. My grandfather, uncle and my mama started work at a factory, the younger ones stayed at home. As time passed the children started to grow in that village named Ivanko. Their house was by a main through way, where people passed by, either to or from the train station, to the village and so life continued.

Hutool (Tribe) people, from where my grandparents came, are very artistic.* **More information about Hutools** If you look it up in the encyclopaedia you will see they had artistic talent, they could draw and paint. For example my grandad and gran could weave baskets they wove different sizes and different types. I remember my gran sat at a spindle spinning yarn; afterwards it would be weaved into material. I also remember them making lace on frames with hooks on them. The family would be engaged in these activities. Children were growing, and so life went on.

A memory has come back to me of Ukrainian customs. Easter, Christmas and Green Easter (Whitsuntide?).

At Whitsun the house was decorated, people went to the woods to collect branches off the trees; also "schebret" was collected. It had a very strong scent and purple small flowers. Its appearance was similar to heather and it spread and grew along the ground. Different flowers and leaves were picked, these were taken to their houses, branches were used to decorate both inside and outside their homes, perfumed flowers were scattered on the window ledges and floors. Bunches of sweet smelling herbs were hung in the rooms. Green Holy Day (Whit) was a lovely happy time to rejoice.

Our Village

This place "Ivanko" was a few kilometres from the nearest market where they went to sell, buy and exchange their goods. They would sell the baskets, or produce, buy what they needed. Sundays were the days for such gathering. Everyone gathered here to meet. Young men and girls got acquainted, a small fair with a carousel was there, it was pleasant, far away from the front line of battle.

My mama had a beau (boyfriend).

Sunday, girls and boys dressed up in their national costumes and off everyone went to the market/fair to buy and sell, to meet and chatter. It was quite a long way to walk to the market from the village. Some went by cart, some rode their horses, others who had no transport walked. That's how my family used to go to the fair/market – they had no horse or cart.

Now! – My mama was a tall attractive woman, dark eyes, long dark thick plaits (long hair on girls was valued), I'm like my father, gingerish hair, small, but I'm not lazy like my father was. Well my mama was noticed by a priest on one of the visits to market. He was young with a long bushy beard, long hair. The first time he noticed her was when they went to the market/fair, the second, third and fourth time. In the end he found out whose daughter she was and went to the village to go to her house.

Gran and grandad were over the moon when he said to them that he really liked their daughter. The grandparents were so happy, they would be wealthy, she would marry a priest, she wouldn't live in poverty. There was a problem though; his mother didn't like the idea. Also the lads kept calling her popadya-popadyouohich, which means priest's wife in a derogatory way. She was young and liked another young man, he also liked her. But the grandparents made it clear, she should be with the priest.

Well, one lovely evening, the moon was shining, stars twinkling over the orchards; it was a beautiful summer's evening. Ukraine has hot summers though sometimes rain, but when the fruit trees blossom what a sight. Then autumn when the leaves begin to show their golden beauty, leaves start to fall, the night grows longer, cold and frost the beginning of winter.

Our winters are very cold with deep snow frost, cold winds, then as the thaw steps in, spring is on its way. You can hear the water bubbling and streaming away, meadows start to show life and flowers start to appear. Perfume is in the air, everyone laughing, birds singing, it's wonderful, especially if you're young, strong and full of that joy of youth.

Back to my story of my mama's courtship.

This beautiful moonlit evening she was sitting in the orchard with the priest suitor, but her heart was heavy as there was no love or joining of souls, but she couldn't go against her parent's wishes. Some boys of the village decided to help out a little. Quietly, they climbed over the fence, crept behind him, grabbed the poor priest and cut his long hair and wonderful bushy beard. The poor man had arrived on his horse and carriage feeling important, because priests were wealthy in those days.

He left, feeling less important, and for a long time was not seen, for to have no long hair and beard was seen as a sin and shame. He did not show himself till his hair and beard had grown. Grandma was very angry with my mama, and she was not allowed to see the young man she liked, as he was the instigator of the incident. That was life in that village named "Ivanki".

Chapter Three

REVOLUTION

Some time passed.

Once more the battle was heading our way over the Ukrainian fields, the front line advancing. Different armies, this army, that army, red army, different groups. My gran said that one group would attack the village plundering, killing those who they thought were with "Spitlooroy"? (Maybe some kind of armed unit). Then men would attack the village for being with the opposite unit. Ivanko was raided by different units, that was war. So! It was forever changing hands. The cruelty of war, the sounds of unhappiness. Voices, shouting, screaming, crying. Whichever political side was in control, still it was the villagers who suffered, most of all the children.

My gran told me of how their house was on fire, one of many in the village. Again they made the decision to move further east. As they went through Uman town they saw fighting there. But they stayed alive and my gran saw the Second World War, though my grandad did not live to see World War 2.

They settled near Uman. Life started again. They had a small house with a large garden and small shed. My mama was growing into a young woman, she was maybe 18/19 years of age? The siblings were also growing up. They worked in a sugar beet factory – my grandad, uncle, mama, whilst gran stayed home to look after the younger children; wove baskets to sell. So life went on, getting used to another part of the country, other customs.

My mama was the eldest, no, her brother was the eldest, she was the eldest daughter when she started getting more interested in boys. She got acquainted with my father, his name was Alexsander or Sasha for short, Sabadir was his surname. He was a charmer and my mama fell in love with him. What his occupation was I really don't know – I was told he was a policeman, but Maroosya my aunt, told Lida when she went there on a visit that he'd been a priest. Maybe he was the priest that had his hair chopped off? (God only knows). Maybe my aunt got it confused.

I still think my father was a policeman, but then I'm told he was a priest, I don't know the truth. No matter how many times I write home (Ukraine) for them to tell me the truth, no one says anything. Aunt Maroosya is old, doesn't remember anything, she says priest! I don't know whom to believe or what.

When a person has a difficult life, hard work, suffering, when a better life comes along then it is easier for them. But when someone has had an easier life, never suffered or seen hardship, when difficult times hit them, some can't bear it.

My father didn't want to work. He was also lazy, so I was told, and not very good to my mama, he'd beat her and had affairs. My grandad hated him. On more than one occasion my grandad threw him out and my mother followed him. I was born in Chistakova which is now Torez. Eventually we returned to Uman.

My mother, grandad, gran (I don't know who else in the family) all worked at the sugar factory, and dad sat at home looking after me. Well at this time, I don't remember my age, but I was a little girl, just starting to walk. They told me that when the sun was hot he would lay in the shade of a tree in the cool. I was left to crawl and toddle about, messy nappies, flies hovering round me. Once I got out of the garden onto the road and a horse and cart ran over me. I have a scar on my forehead from that incident; this was told to me by my aunts. It was a great shock to my grandparents. They beat him.

Well I was growing. I was still very young, maybe 3 or 4, when my grandad threw my father out again. My mother took me though, against grandad's wishes, got a cart and went with my father back to the Donbas, which was an industrial region, the distance to travel was about 1000 kilometres.

Once again my mother was wandering. With a husband that was unreliable, lazy, no good but she took her small child Katya (that's me) and off she went to the Donbas. When they arrived in the Donbas, they found themselves lodgings and hired themselves out as cowherds. This is how it was. Everyone in the village who had a cow, at break of day, herded the cow onto a field. A couple of cowherds who'd been hired then came herding the cows together and took them to pasture, in different fields and valleys. They hired themselves out for this work.

My dad would lay in the shade whilst my poor mother with bare feet used to chase round after the cows, through grass, brambles and thorns. My father would sit under a tree minding me. It became too much for my mother, so once again they returned to their Uman, to her parents.

Naturally, my grandparents were overjoyed to see their first grandchild and let them stay. A short time passed and again my father would have a job then leave, the problems started again. My mother gave birth to a little boy the name of my little brother was Vasya. One day he was being rocked by my father in a cradle, this cradle was fastened to the ceiling, somehow, Vasya tried to get up, the cradle up tipped, his head was dashed on the hard floor, he fell ill then died. This made my grandparents even more bitter, towards their son in law, who they didn't love.

There was nothing to love about him, he was a thief, but I always thought of him, he was my father, I remember him. But I think if my son in law behaved like that, I also would have rejected him.

Before he was ordered out of the house, they went to Dnepepetrovsk to visit, because he was from there. He didn't seem to have any relatives, only an old woman, maybe an aunt, I don't know. They stayed with this aunt, whether she was a blood aunt or just someone who had reared him, God knows. She had icons in the house, my mama had to prostrate herself on the floor, kiss and pray to the icons morning and evening. Eventually she had enough and returned back to her parents.

Again everyone was working and my father sat at home. My grandad threw him out once more but my mother didn't want to go with him, because grandad said, "I'm not letting Katya go with you, you both go out into the world, go where you want but I'm not letting the child go with you to suffer". What happened? My father had to leave my mother as she would not leave me, she had to live with what fate had dealt her, she stayed with her parents.

I have a memory of our parting. We were in the barn where hay was stored, sat high on a wide rafter swinging our legs. He embraced me and said "Katya your grandad doesn't want me here, I'm going to go to the Donbas get work in the coal mines, earn a lot of money, come back for you and your mum. I'll buy you a lovely dress and your mum a beautiful scarf". So that was how we parted, he went off to the Donbas. It is a shame to speak ill of the dead, but what can I say but the truth. I was told he went to the Donbas to work in the coalmines.

The miners who were not local, lived in barracks. My father and his friend got drunk and somehow set fire to the barrack. When the workers returned home and saw their hard got possessions were ashes, the miners started to beat them, and then threw them near to a river bank; and that was the last that was ever heard of my father.

When I was 18 I tried to find out more about what happened to my dad. I wrote everywhere including the newspapers but never found out anything.

Our family continued their lives. One particular time I was startled and frightened (I was only a small child) by the shouting that was going off in the house. What it was was my aunt, my mother's sister was courting a militia man, a friend of my fathers and she had got pregnant, that was what the mayhem was about. Everyone was shouting, crying, swearing. My grandma had got my Aunt Lena and was pulling her by the hair, beating her. I as a small child looked on frightened. Grandad wasn't at home, I didn't know what was happening. My grandma had Aunt Lena pinned near the fireplace, her sisters were shouting at her and crying, because she had brought great shame on the family by getting pregnant and not being married. Anyway, she got married to this Pavel Barahalenko. He wasn't worth much, as he was lazy like my father, like a lot of militia men. That's what I remember.

Time went on, eventually they all decided to move to the Donbas* (put information about Donbas at the back), to the coalmines. We arrived in the Donbas by train; all the family arrived and rented a small house. Again it was a garden yard with 2 houses (I've forgotten the name of the other people).

Again a similar life began. Weaving baskets, carving out wooden dishes and spoons. I know how to weave baskets I have a bit of a talent for weaving baskets (Mama goes on to explain how). They were engaged in buying and selling. Grandad and Uncle Vasya used to travel to Uman where they had contacts. Dried fruits were brought back, sacks of dried cherries, apricots, plums, apples in sacks; in exchange they sold their wares. The produce was then sold in the mining areas. These trading journeys were made by train.

One of my aunts was married at this time, the other aunts were too young to marry, but helped my grandma weaving. My mother worked at the coal mine like a lot of girls and women. Those days they worked down the mine or on the pit top (as they did in Britain in the Victorian/olden days), men and women were supposed to be equal.

Chapter Four

MY STEPFATHER

My mama got acquainted with my future stepfather, his name was Grigory Zagarodny. Now I'll tell you about my stepdad. He came from the Vinitsi area; a place named Lipovti, his father was a wealthy miller. His Mum was a big woman, she was tall and good looking and rich. In 1932/33 she came to visit with her boyfriend, as her husband had died. She came at the time of the famine when thousands of people died from hunger. She caused my mama many problems. My stepdad also had a sister?

Grandma Anna and Step-Grandad Grigory with his mother on her visit to them in 1932-33

Stepfather was educated and artistic, very clever, carpenter, mechanic, electrician – he could do anything. He made guitars, furniture, anything he put his hands to he could do. His father, being rich, sent him to learn different kinds of crafts. He was still single but had a girlfriend in Vinitsc who his parents wanted him to marry. She was rich, but he didn't want to marry her. He came to the Donbas a wealthy, talented, handsome man.

He lived at his uncles, his uncle worked at Pit No 6 Cashelovka. He got acquainted with my mother as they both worked at the mine and then fell in love with her. They started meeting, courting, in secret, as it would upset the family, as 2 younger sisters and brother were not married, so it was not appropriate to marry a second time when younger siblings were still single. Another reason my gran and grandad didn't want my mama to marry became clearer later. My mother started to seek her husband, my father Sasha Sabadir, to get a divorce putting adverts in the newspapers. She tried everything, but nothing was heard of him, but after 6 or 7 years of being on her own she was given a divorce, she was freed from him.

Mother worked at the coalmine, she was a lovely woman, tall, handsome. She was a quiet woman, couldn't sing, dance, read or write, but! he fell in love with her. Life trickled on; I was loved by my grandparents, aunts and uncles. Also I was spoilt, as I was the first grandchild.

Now I'm going to tell you about my mama's marriage.

One beautiful evening, the sun was just starting to set, a cool breeze was just starting to blow. Summer can be very hot in the Donbas. As evening came, people started to appear. Some were bringing their cows from the fields. Peoples' laughter, chatter floated through the air, the moo, moo, moo of the cows mingling amongst the evening sounds. Children running round, laughing and shouting.

I was playing out in the yard. When I looked I saw mama with a strange man, walking towards the house, along the street. He was very handsome, a big fella, smashing. I ran into the cottage, grandma was sat roasting/frying sunflower and pumpkin seeds, because this was another produce we sold. I loved my gran and grandad but grandad was rarely at home. On this occasion he was away with my uncle Vasya selling basket ware and buying dried fruits in Kiev. Gran was roasting sunflower seeds and in walked the stranger with my mother. He greets my gran "good evening", "good evening" she answered. (He once told me that he thought gran had an idea why he was there).

I was sitting next to my gran; he politely said "I've come to ask whether I can marry your daughter Anna?" Gran jumped up in anger. She was small but had a temper. "She's already been married, look at the result" she shouted, pointing at me. He started calmly to try and talk her round. "I know she's been married, I know she has a daughter, but I want to marry your daughter." I was hiding behind my gran, peeping round wondering what was happening. Gran started shouting like a madwoman. "You may have a wife and children, you may be a rogue! I don't know anything about you!" He calmly answered "I'm not a rogue I'm from a respectable family, a mother, a father, my uncle lives in this area, I have no wife."

He continued patiently to placate my gran; she refused to calm down and continued shrieking. He lost his patience, banged on the table with his fist, looked at my mama and said "Anna, are you coming with me or staying with your mama?" She looked at him and quietly answered "I'm going with you." "Are you going to marry me, or stay here with your mother?"

As was the custom, my gran over the years had been preparing a bottom drawer where you put away household linen, crockery, cutlery etc for the bride as a dowry. This was given to the daughter on the day of her marriage. Of course gran had unmarried daughters at home. Gran started screeching again, "I'm giving you nothing, nothing! You can go with just the clothes on your back!"

He listened to all this and said. "She doesn't need anything from you", he angrily thumped the table with his fist and again asked, "Are you going to marry me, or stay with your mother?" She answered "marry you". "Let's go" he said and took my mama's hand. I grabbed my gran's skirt, my gran was holding onto me as my mum was trying to talk me into going with them, tugging at me, I was crying, distraught. I think I was maybe 9/10 at the time. My future stepdad had had enough; he grabbed me and put me on his shoulders. Gran was distressed, shouting, waving her fists and swearing at them; and off we went.

The sun was just setting, a summer evening, perfumed with blossom and flowers of the gardens and orchards, apples pears, cherries, lilacs. Roses that flowered in the gardens. The streets that ran through the village were straight dirt roads, no tarmac or pavements. We kept walking on, with me crying, trying to break away, pleading, "I want my grandma." We seemed to be walking a long way, eventually we arrived. The house where we arrived at was one my stepdad was building for a man, next to one he had built for someone else. By trade he was a mechanic, but as I said earlier, he was a clever man and could put his hand to most things. (If he lived here in England, he would be a millionaire).

We entered the empty unfurnished house, most of it was finished only there were no doors or glass in the windows, but this did not matter as it was summer and warm, and a lot of people took their mattresses and slept outside on warm summer nights. Off my mama and stepdad went, bringing back with them bundles of hay which was placed on the floor beneath the window. The house had nothing in it apart from the straw, well, we only stayed in it a couple of days.

The next thing he did was to go to his lodgings to collect his clothes and possessions. His landlady was a wealthy woman, a tailoress, she got upset that he was leaving and refused to give him his things. Now whether there was a romance between them, I don't know, but he'd fallen in love with mama and wanted to marry her. Well he came back with a couple of blankets and covered the hay and we lay down to sleep.

I was still very distraught, and lay crying, I wanted to be with my gran! With my grandad! How could it be I was not? Mama lay trying to comfort me, but I was inconsolable. The sadness and loneliness I felt stayed in my heart, for the things that are done to a child, stays in the memory, as it has stayed with me, to this day.

Next morning we arose early. Again I started crying, wanting my grandparents. My stepdad went out. Later we saw him returning, walking down the street with a large pack on his shoulders. He had bought clothes for my mama, clothes for me and different household goods. He obviously loved my mother, he approached her, embraced her. She had a dress on with grey pinstripes, which he ripped off her and threw it away. Mother was then dressed in all new clothes; they picked a posy of flowers and went off to the Gorod Soviet (Town Hall). There they registered their marriage, and came back married. I have a photo of their marriage that I got when I went home.

My stepfather asked for a transfer to another pit about 5 miles away, and we moved to another village. There they rented a house from a Mr Hrunich. It was a small house with 2 rooms, kitchen, larder and corridor as I remember. Two or 3 steps to enter this little house.

My parents started to brew "samahon" which is a home made vodka. Though it was illegal it was a common practice. They sold this samahon. They used to hide massive bottles, maybe 2 gallons in size, digging holes in the orchard and hiding them there. If the police found out they would be summonsed. I used to sleep on the floor, near to the distiller. This particular time, I don't know how, but the steam that came out scalded my leg. I still have the scars to this day. When the steam scalded me, I screamed. All my leg was covered in blisters from top to bottom. I remember they rubbed goose grease on to try and help. I don't remember any doctor coming.

I may tell you some more of this later.

My stepdad worked at the pit while mother stayed at home. One day I was outside the house when I saw a horse and carriage with a man in it. He wasn't very tall, nice looking and well built. I shouted to my mama that there someone was coming. Mama knew who it was as it was her ex boyfriend. He was the son of close friends of gran and grandad who were Austro Hungarian refugees like them. He had been courting my mama but had gone to college. My mama was supposed to wait for him. She couldn't get married at this time because she had to wait a few years before she could get a divorced.

He had been sent to the pit to work as an engineer and had managed to get our address. He came into the house with a bottle of vodka and they started to talk. Then my stepfather came home from work. He introduced himself to my stepfather and asked why "did you take my girl, she was supposed to wait for me?" They talked and parted on good terms. I realised that this was part of the reason gran and grandad didn't want my mama to remarry.

A decision was made by them to start breeding pigs in the yard. There was a shed. They started breeding and selling pigs, this gave them a good standard of life.

I was a very jealous child and couldn't stand my stepdad because he'd taken me and my mother away from my grandparents. Mama told me to call him Papa but I couldn't think of him as a father for a long, long time. Time passed. My mother was homesick. Her husband said to her "I didn't force you; you came of your own will!"

Grigory and Anna Zagarodni lived well. He made furniture, played the harmonium and guitar. They loved one another, but my mama still cried for her home. Her mother, my gran, didn't want anything to do with her; although my aunts, her younger sisters, used to pretend they were going swimming in the river, or to the cinema, then run like mad to visit us so gran wouldn't know.

I hated my stepdad for taking us away from grans. My mama loved her husband very much. I was resentful and felt not much love or gentleness, but then in those days, not much affection was shown. The tenderness you received was the tenderness of a stick or belt if you misbehaved. Tenderness, not much

Grandma Anna and Step-Grandad Grigory playing accordion

of it, but beatings, there were enough of those.

One day I went into the orchard, not ours, but next doors. We didn't have any apple trees, only plums, but he had apple trees. I was only a child, and found the apples inviting, so I climbed over the fence, then grabbed a branch to get an apple – the branch broke. The owner, Mr Hrunich came out with a look of thunder, grabbed me and threw me over the fence, and not short a distance. My mum came out and he started shouting, complaining about me. She got so angry with me, why had I gone there? She grabbed me, there was a rope lying near by. She thrashed me till the neighbours got her off me. Well, well, all type of things happened in childhood. When it's a second marriage. Well that's why I never got married again. No one was going to beat my children. Now they're all adults, it's my business what I do.

Life trickled on. Then one day we received a telegram. My beloved grandad had died. I shed many tears, he loved me so and I knew it.

Remembering when my mum was leaving home, gran had shouted "I'm giving you nothing of the dowry." My stepdad had turned round to her answering "She neither wants nor needs anything from you, she'll come to you for nothing." "You will need us first" and that's as it was. My old gran lived to see his words fulfilled.

We went to grandad's funeral. The custom was to have an open coffin in the house, so everyone could come and say goodbye. I wept many tears, out of this sadness. My mama and gran were reunited after the funeral. Plans were made for us to go back to be near my gran. My mother was so happy to be returning.

Land was being distributed in Chestakova (Torez). Stepdad got some land at the bottom of the street from where gran lived with her unmarried son Fyeda, single daughters Nyoosya and Maria. In time Gran would come to live with us. On this plot he built a lovely house, although it was small. Three rooms, kitchen, veranda and a kitchen outside which was used for cooking in the summer months. I'll try and describe the place of my youth.

Grandma Anna and Grandad Grigory's house rebuilt after the war

The streets were in diagonal lines with small houses and orchards on either side. At the top of the streets were older houses, then the new development carried on where the new settlement continued. Recently when I returned after maybe 50 years, the houses have been built as far as the river.

Eventually the fields came into view, dipping down into a small valley, where a wide river flowed. Crossing the river again there were fields rising. (Info Chistakova Glossary) As you got to the top, pits and coal tips (spoil heaps) came into view. Our people love nature, flowers in our house. We had a carpet (tapestry) hung on the wall, a ficus that grew up to the ceiling, also a landra, a gramophone was in the room along with a guitar and harmonica. Mama and stepdad used to go to celebrations like weddings to play his music.

Auntie Nyoosya got married, uncle Fyeda married a girl named Nadya, two of my aunt's married militia men (police) like my blood father. The family all got together and built them small cottages. These were built on similar lines to the Carpathian houses, but they had slates not thatch. At our place we had a cow, chickens, geese, ducks, turkeys, pigs we had everything. We had an allotment in a field nearby and another allotment in another valley, maybe 2 or 3 miles from the house.

Chapter Five

MUM'S CHILDHOOD

(Our mama Katya is eating as she tells the next part, lips smacking can be heard).

Now I'm going to tell you about my childhood.

My childhood was gloomy, sad. First I'd lost my father, then my grandad, whom I loved very much died. Another thing – my mama remarried, loved her husband, had 4 children with him, Mitya, Valya, Victor, Alexander (Sasha). I felt like an orphan, felt lonely. I wanted kindness. Someone to hold me, and show gentleness, as I had seen in my friend's families, but I felt alone. I know other people had, and have, a more difficult childhood, but I'm writing my grievances, as now I have more time to think and (write) tell about this.

One of my chores was to go to the allotments, one near the river in the valley, one in the field, to water the vegetables. The allotment near the river was about 2 miles from home, there we grew things like tomatoes, cabbage, green pepper and gherkins. Each plant had to have half a bucket of water and it would often be very late when I returned home, but I always felt safe. It was a pleasant walk, in warm months as I used to go barefoot. When the moon shone bright you could see maybe 20 kilometres over the valley to the coalmines, flames flickering in the distance.

Our house as I've said before was cosy. In the garden there were acacias, lilac and roses which could be seen through the window, asters and marigolds in patches. An apricot grew, spreading its branches in the front garden. The back yard was tidy and laid out in stone. Also at the back were sheds where our livestock was kept. My parents and gran all toiled hard. I being the eldest also had to take on the burden with them. As a young child I was always unhappy, always tired as everyone worked hard. So did I, even though I was a thin bony child.

Mama Katya in tears

They were very strict, also I think I was in the way, and many arguments between them were because of me. Then my mama would beat me, taking her anger out on me for doing some minor misdemeanour. I was only a child. On one occasion, we were at the allotment near the river. I was given a key and told to go home to fetch something they'd forgotten. The house was quite a distance.

I arrived home, put the key in the lock and it wouldn't open, so I got a nail, pushed it in, trying to force the key. Yes! That's right the door opened, but I'd broken the key. I knew I would be beaten for this, so I hid in the haystack, making a small peephole, where I could watch the house. My parents had finished their work and, as I hadn't returned, they came home, saw the door open and a broken key. They realised I'd got frightened and had run off. They started looking for me, but couldn't find me.

Meanwhile, I'd made a cosy spot in the hay, with my peephole I could keep watch. Evening came, I watched as they all sat round the table for their evening meal. I felt such a feeling of sadness. At the same time relief they had not found me, so at least I had not been beaten. I hid all next day. By chance the neighbour had seen me when I crept out, so told my mama. Of course when she found me, the beating was more severe than if I'd have stayed and owned up that I'd broken the key.

Another incident I remember breaking a plate with the same result, beaten. Mama and stepdad were always arguing about me. My aunt told me recently she used to say to my mother "Anna, why are so demanding of her? She's only a small child to be laden with all those chores." "Ah", my mother answered, "work never harmed anyone; I also have to work hard."

Another beating was for breaking a needle in the singer sewing machine. I was trying to sew, the needle pierced my finger and I broke the needle. Of course these needles were difficult to get. I covered the singer machine, hoping it would not be seen. No such luck. Again I was punished, again I ran off, again my mama found me.

One memory follows another. I'm remembering events from my school years, some of which were very traumatic.

One day, me and my friends, were walking home from school. We walked through a copse looking for damsons. Suddenly we saw the figure of a man hanging from a tree. We ran screaming. People came and we found out later that he had been coming home from work with his wages and was robbed and hanged.

I recall another incident. One day coming home from school, instead of going straight home we went another route trying to be clever climbing over the fence. Suddenly we saw hands and legs. Screaming we ran away. When people went back it was someone run down by a train.

Another memory. One day we went to collect the cows from the fields, there was a quarry on our way back where everyone used to swim. I could see all the others swimming, so I thought I'd start swimming even though I didn't know how. I jumped in and went under the deep water. I kept coming up and then going under again. Everyone thought I was diving and kept saying "Oooh! look at her diving". Then my friend who was a little bit older than me realised that I was drowning. She got hold of my hand and I grabbed her by her hair and started climbing on top of her. It's a TERRIBLE experience when you're drowning. It's horrible when you're gasping for breath and keep going back under. Anyway someone jumped from the top and grabbed us both by the hair and pulled us out. They started pumping the water out of me. I nearly died then.

A couple of years later another tragic scene. We were coming home from school and we saw plenty of people they were saying that there'd been an explosion at the pit. Being children we clambered to the front. I'll never forget it. It looked like pieces of burnt wood. These were bodies that had been burnt in the explosion. This was about 1932.

Gosh my life. All my life death followed me, everywhere I go and I'm still living, thank you God. I'm still alright and my mind hasn't gone curva, sorry I'm swearing (Ukrainian swear word).

But I had pleasant memories as well.

I used to love reading, especially poetry, Vinichenko, Ivan Franko, Kobzar Shevchenko (Ukrainian National Poet). I loved to read romantic stories. I remember reading a novel about a girl Katarina who got pregnant so was chased away from home and hounded out of the village for being pregnant and not married. She went from place to place but no one wanted her with a child. (and that was our sex education! Not the birds and bees – Lid).

Another episode. We were always scaring people with ghosts. One day my friend and I were waiting for the cows to be returned. I got a white blanket and waited until everyone came back with the cows. I put the white blanket over my head, stretched out my arms and began walking behind the bushes in the cemetery. If you could have seen them (mama chuckles) one old woman went running in one direction and we ran in another direction and came out of the cemetery. Do you know everyone was talking about a ghost being in the cemetery. We didn't tell anyone or my mama would have killed me!

Flour Mill in Chistakova (Torez) Spring 1930? Grandma Anna with babe in arms Auntie Valya (bottom row far right) Behind Grandma Anna's left shoulder (far right) Step-Grandad Grigory inembroidered shirt

Mama and stepdad lived together happily. My mama always dressed nice when they went anywhere. She had a beautiful shawl/scarf; her hair was thick and plaited. I watched as they kidded and embraced each other. This made me more jealous, hating my stepfather even more. I was 12 years of age when they had their first child.

I used to have to take the cow to pasture in the field and wait for the cowherd to collect her. I used to rise early, maybe 4.00am, walking to the edge of the village, then into the valley where the river flowed. Not far away from the river were fields of sunflowers and sweetcorn. I'd sit under the sunflowers, barefoot, cold, the dew still on the ground. Huddled up with my head on my knees. I'd drop to sleep.

Meanwhile the cow would wander off. When I awoke, I started running, searching through the maize and yellow flowers calling her name, "Manya, Manya, Manya" I'd find her, the cowherd arrived collecting the cow taking the herd to new pastures, returning at noon to the homesteads. The cows were milked and he would collect them to take to pasture. In the evening we had to collect the cow, mama or me, because dad was always busy. Mostly it was I who collected the cow from the field where the cowherd had returned her to. Sometimes when there were storms, the cows were returned early, and then the owners would have to collect them.

I was a poor little thing. I remember running soaked with the rain, barefooted, thunder crashing, lightening crackling, but I was never afraid.

Mama Katya wasn't afraid in her youth of storms, though after the war, storms and the noise frightened her.

Another thing I remember.

The winters were harsh. School was some distance away through fields. I was late from school one day and Dad was worried and decided to come looking for me. He walked through a field and saw a large lump of snow and found me underneath. If he hadn't found me this story would not now be told. I remember just wanting to sleep; it would be the easiest death, go to sleep and that's it!

My mother gave birth to her first child from her second husband. It was Xmas time, snow lay on the ground, crisp. We children were running round the village, carol singing from house to house. For our carols we received sweets, biscuits or kopecks (small change) or nuts, and then took our gifts home. New Year we scattered grain all over, so the coming year would be successful.

My mama baked, cooked, sewed, looked after the livestock. Father also worked hard, he worked at the coalmine, but was hardly ever home as he did other jobs. Putting windows in, carpentry, he even made furniture. We lived pretty well, but my childhood was sad. That's how I know rich parents can give their children material wealth but if they haven't love and kindness they have nothing.

Another memory I have was of a family who lived opposite us a family called Zhuravetch. I was about 12/13 at the time. Mr Zhuravetch was a big fat fella reminds me of someone I know (Uncle Victor?). When it was pay day he would get vodka, salami, bread. He would walk through the village. You could see him from a long way, talking and singing with his friends, already drunk. He had about 5/6 kids. The kids would be happy with sweets. As it got dark he would beat his wife, the kids would run screaming to hide at the neighbours.

We lived very well, we had plenty of food that we stored in the cellar and attic. The cellars were situated in the garden, sometimes the kitchen. There was a trapdoor that lifted open, with ladders leading underground where produce was stored. As it was dark and cool, vegetables etc would keep longer. When mama went to the market and gran was busy doing other things I would steal food and take it to them. They were very poor and had nothing. I was caught by gran and mama on many occasions and I often would get a big hiding. I remember one day I had lots of dry fruit in my pockets and was just going across the road when my gran caught me. I got yet another hiding.

Now what shall I tell you, now I'll start.

Maybe it was Holy Night (Christmas Eve). Everything was being prepared for the meal, so that we sat down as the sun set. A pig had been slaughtered as was the custom on feast days. Salamis were made, brawn and different dishes prepared, bread and pasties were baked. My stepfather was a good worker. He went to clean the cowsheds feed the pigs; get all the outdoor chores finished, before dusk.

Everything was cheerful, evening came, we were preparing to sit down for our feast, when my gran took me to my aunts. I didn't know why. Of course it was my mother preparing to give birth. Stepfather got the sledge and horse prepared them for a journey to the town, to the hospital.

It was a clear moonlit night, so bright, no lights were needed; you appeared to be able to see miles. It was a frosty night, the snow lay white, so clean, my stepfather wrapped my mama up in a feather down quilt (called a pirina in Ukrainian language), put her on the sledge and set off on their journey. The snow was very deep; the horse sank one leg into the snow, then the other leg. The poor horse was struggling, the bright moon appeared to be chuckling, as if he thought "what on earth are you doing, you'll not get to the hospital or anywhere else", as it was, the moon was right.

Stepfather decided to return to the village to take the horse back and replace him with 2 fresh horses. There was a Kolhoz (commune farm) near the village. He unharnessed the horse from the sledge, leaving mama in the sledge, alone in the countryside, he went back.

As he was returning with 2 fresh horses, he heard screams; it was my mama with no one there to hear her pain. Only the wind howling through the fields she was giving birth to our Valya there in the snow swept fields. As stepdad approached he was shouting to her, "hold on I'm here". My mama was shouting for him to hurry. As he arrived he realised that it was too late. Valya was born. After he had helped with the birth, he harnessed the horses and returned to the village. They went to my uncle's house; my gran lived there at this time. Mama stayed to rest.

The next morning they took me to see the baby. "Katya, come and look what a beautiful sister you have", they said. They took me to her. I looked at her, my first feelings were I didn't like her at all; she was so red with black hair. I really didn't like her, jealousy you see.

Life continued, but now I had to look after Valya. I always had her with me. If I had spare time, of course there were other chores. We had a floor that had been painted in red lacquer paint. When I scrubbed the floor my mother used to inspect it even under the table to make sure I hadn't missed any of the floor. Many times I pretended to be asleep to get out of washing the pots. I hated the job; my mama would wake me all the same. Don't forget there was no running water so it had to be brought from the river, and then heated on the stove. Winter we used to use snow that we melted.

That's why my children are so clean and I am particular as they say in England. I'd rather leave the mess where it's seen than try and hide it under the table or bed. That's how I was taught from childhood.

Toilets were in the garden at the bottom, a hut was built and a hole dug out. No electric, we used kerosene lamps for light, washing clothes; they were boiled and scrubbed on a stone or with a brush.

For winter we always prepared different pickles and conserves. Autumn was the season when produce was picked, barrels of cabbage was salted, gherkins, aubergines, tomatoes were also put into the barrels and preserved. If you didn't grow or have enough to conserve for the winter, when autumn arrived there came into the village large wagons where produce could be bought. Everything was homemade, jams with different fruit, mushrooms were dried, also apples, pears, plums, cherries everything was your own efforts.

Ukrainian fields and woods are lovely. Orchards, little whitewashed houses, all people whether they were Ukrainian, Poles or Russians loved embroidery. A lot of the items in the houses were embroidered cushions, bedspreads and pillowcases. Houses were whitewashed inside and out. The sun shone. Such wonderful perfumes wafted from the fields and woods.

So we lived well our family but my poor aunt who was married to a millitionare (policeman) it was not so. When he worked things weren't too bad, when he decided not to work times were hard. He was the type of person that winter time was too cold to work and summer time too hot, my poor aunt had to work, she also had 3 children to take care of. She got pneumonia and died. Halya one of her daughters came to live with us. She was killed in the war, when our house was bombed, of which I'll tell you later.

My mother had more children, we were all growing.

Chapter Six

MUM YOUNG ADULT

Well what else have I to tell you.

I started work as a cashier in one shop then progressed to another shop. Meanwhile I was studying. I eventually got a job as an assistant to the deputy manager in a village co-op, I wasn't there long. One of my duties was to check the stock; we sold all sorts, salamis, bread, materials and so forth. I trusted the girls I worked with, so I didn't really check as much as I should have done. Somehow they had managed to fiddle me, the result being I had 300 roubles, (I think) to repay, but not in money but in work.

I was sent to work in a coalmine. I arrived at the barracks that housed the workers. There were groups of girls laughing, talking, joking, but for me it was very difficult. That I'd walked so tall and had fallen so low through someone else's actions, this taught me a lesson not to trust so easily. My days at the mine began.

If you worked in the mine it wasn't so bad as it was warm. Empty wagons were fastened then sent to the coalface, then you had to go to the coalface attach the wagons again and sent them to the top. Working on the pit top the conditions were tougher. Coal came along a conveyer belt, under the conveyor stood the wagons where the coal was sorted by size into the wagons. When a wagon was full you had to push it away to a field. In winter it was so cold our feet were wrapped in rags pushing these wagons not just me, others as well.

When evening came I'd go back to the barracks some girls had boyfriends, others would be sat laughing and joking. Remember this was not a prison, just an ordinary working mine. I'd sit on my own, feeling so down and alone, I didn't want to mix with anyone. I used to think; when I've worked my time I'll leave and go to the end of the earth where no one knows me.

My parents were well off when I fell into this disgrace through no fault of mine, no one wanted to know. No one came to see me, only one uncle. My mother was too afraid of my father; he was well known and didn't want to be connected to my problem. I paid off my debt in toil and left the mine.

I went far away to the Caucuses to my godmothers.

*It hurt my heart so much that my mother didn't contact me. I said to myself if ever I have children I would never leave them. Be there for them in troubles no matter what, I'd kill to protect them.

I arrived in the Caucuses, a place unknown to me. All I had with me was an address, a couple or roubles and my pass papers. I had travelled through Rostov, Kuban, Armavir and found myself in Nalchik. Nalchik is a most beautiful place set between the mountains. Elbrooz, the high peak being not far away. I arrived at my godmother's house. They were amazed to see me; I wanted to be far away from anyone I knew. They didn't want me when I was in trouble, so I didn't want anyone now, only to forget them all.

My first job was in a pump house (garage). Nalchik had many different peoples, it felt exotic. Georgian, Ossetians, Karbardans etc. Hot water flowed down the mountains, hot enough to scold, it bubbled down the rocks into streams. Across the river you could see small houses made of straw, they were called "Aooli" where the Karbardans and Ossetians lived. The women of these people were very beautiful, but soon looked worn out with their hard lives. Mostly the men looked after the sheep or saw to the fields, the women did most of the work.

Their culture allowed a man to have more than one wife. Now under Soviet rule, this was not allowed. Still it was common practice when a wife aged; the husband would take a younger woman, who would bear him more children. The first wife helped look after them. I was really enjoying life in Nalchik. I had pleasant comradeship with Russians and Ukrainians.

At the petrol pump station I used to meet drivers, but I wasn't interested, as I had hopes of building a better life for myself. Previously when I was younger I had been to medical school. After about a year I left, I couldn't go on. Then next I tried a course at the technical college and learnt to be a typist, but then I didn't want that job. Then a cashier, that result was I worked the coal mine, ending up in the Caucuses.

In Nalchik I decided to go to evening school. I also got involved in a small way in politics. I joined the Komsomol (communist youth – similar to girl guides and scouts but with political intonations). I was very patriotic, I loved my motherland. I also went to learn parachuting.

Time passed pleasantly and I got a job. A carabnier? (security guard) who used to look after the gates took a liking to me. Every time I passed the petrol station he would try and flirt with me. I just couldn't bear anyone touching me. He tried to hold my hand, many a time I'd say to him "leave me alone, leave me alone, don't touch me". One time I was angry and got a bucket of cold water that was stood near by and threw it at him. This incident was at work so I had to be punished. I was taken to court and made to pay a fine. It was a trifle so it didn't bother me. It was worth it.

Nalchik, (which is the Turkish name for a horseshoe), was a lovely place as I said before, with its mountains, river running through, small Aooli (cottages/tents) made of straw. A pleasant park in the town where people walked, children played, summer evening music and singing drifted in the air. We lived just outside the town where the meat conserve factory was, and had to cross fields to get there.

I never walked alone; we were always in groups, lads and lasses. A drama circle was in the town which I took part in. I played roles on stage, sang, I had a good voice, was enjoying life, but still I was not content.

My next job was an instructor for the Red Cross near Nalchik. It was an important job. I used to visit schools, universities, organising different groups. I met people who were up a notch, life was good. Life was smiling at me, but I wanted to see more of the world. The next incident gave me the opportunity.

A good friend of mine Maryoosya was going out with the chief of the police. My other friend was going out with an "affirist (a swindler) who took part in shady dealings. He forged money or documents etc. His dealings were up in the hills of Nalchik. The swindlers got caught. I was not aware of what was going on. Maryoosya and Nadya had to make a getaway, they decided on Nikolayev. She wrote a letter to me telling me what a wonderful place Nikolayev was, asking for me to go there. Nikolayev was where my uncle's sister lived, that is my aunt's husband's sister. So I see my papers are in order, leave my job and go. Now I arrive in Nikolayev.

It was a nice place, but Maryoosya had no where to stay. On her arrival she'd got acquainted with some people who gave her a place to stay. She lived in a grave yard, old trees, tombs (mausoleums) like small houses you could enter. It was an old grave yard, opposite was a market and at the entrance were 2 small buildings, one of which had been a mortuary where corpses were kept. Anyway this was the room which these people gave Maryoosya to live in. When I arrived in Nikolayev I found my relative, then later found my friend and discovered where she lived. Evenings I used to visit her in the graveyard. The market opposite was on Vaenaya Street.

When I went to visit her it was a bit scary. People sat near their homes (mausoleums) as if it was nothing. When the frosts came I recall looking down at the river that in the moonlight appeared as if silver was flowing. There were 2 or 3 grave yards further on. I lived further on from the grave yards and had to go round to try to pass them. Although there were times when I was brave and went through them.

I carried on with my friendship with Maryoosya. Life at Nikolayev was good, but I don't want to dwell on trivia. I want to get to my life in the war and the labour camps and prison.

I was young, beautiful with blonde hair and wherever I went I could get a cavalier (admirer/boyfriend), but I was not interested. The reason being, when I was 12 I was left with a boy of 16, he raped me. I was very ill. No one knew what was wrong with me. My mum put warm wheat bags on my stomach, gave me tablets. Fear is a terrible thing. I dare not tell anyone as he had said, "If you tell anyone what has happened, I will cut your throat". When I went outside into our yard he would mime slashing my throat, this was very frightening.

Back to my story.

Nikolayev had a river estuary. A village was situated on the other side of the river. Walking along the river banks in the evening girls singing could be heard from the village across the river. Evenings in town were pleasant. Women and men in groups joking, laughing, chatting. Music could be heard drifting from the park. In the evenings, mothers, fathers, children enjoyed strolling in the park. It was a place people met, pleasant.

My memories are of how we used to gather in the evenings in each others houses. Then, there was no electricity; people rose early, just as dawn was breaking, and lay down to sleep at nightfall. This was the older generation, but the young – oh the young people! When their parents went to bed, they came out onto the streets and started singing and dancing. At our place it was lovely; moonlit nights, warm evenings; many slept outdoors, but I'll tell you about that later.

Below, where the river ran was a popular place at weekends and holidays. A sandy beach ran alongside of the river. There children played, people sunbathed or swam. Boats could be hired, where you could row across to the opposite bank, where reeds grew, a haven for birds, herons, wild geese etc. Nikolayev had some very nice places, and so life passes like a bubbling stream, happy and content.

I was in the komsomol (young communist's league). This helped me get a job as a secretary at the town hall, where it led to my second job at the "politprosoviet" (political education system). I was so proud when I was requested to work as secretary to the regional deputy of soviets in the bureau of complaints. The building stood in front of a large square where demonstrations took place. This is where I met the man who was to become my first husband, Sasha Demenschenko?

He was older than me and had just left the army, he was an engineer. I was to know gentleness and respect by the way he treated me. Sasha's mother had died giving birth to him so he'd been brought up by an aunt whom he called mother. Our courtship began; he was very good to me.

When I visited, his "mama" used to say "Sasha, be good to her she's so nice". I was a sweet girl (Lid adds – modest too!) but I could be strong also.

My beloved first husband Sasha. We married April 1940. He was killed aged 25 years of age.
(I am on the right.)

It was April when we wed, at the register office with just a couple of friends present. Life was shining, we were happy. We lived in a small room with a tiny kitchen in the area "sadovi" gardens as it was known, we were content. It was the month of June 1941, or July I think, I've forgotten, we came home and were told "the Germans have attacked the motherland." Everyone became frightened.

Chapter Seven

THE BEGINNING OF THE WAR

Arriving at his aunt's house she told us the radio has just transmitted that the enemy is attacking our Ukraine. Bombs have fallen on some towns. The evening was so beautiful. The moon shining, scents from the gardens, but everywhere there was silence, people were frightened, wondering what the future held, that fear embraced everyone. Those who had experienced wars, they had an idea of what was ahead. We the younger generation were so patriotic; I was going to become a nurse.

To be honest, we should have realised trouble was ahead, as for a couple of months we had been training to defend the town. Fire drills were more than usual. Here begins a horrible, awful, frightening life. That was my childhood sadness, unhappiness, moments of joy, moments of anger, moments that were good.

Life in the Caucuses had been fulfilling and joyful. Now in Nikolayev, I'm young, energetic, have a loving husband. At the start of the war there were no attacks or bombing in Nikolayev. You maybe heard an explosion now and again, in the distance, or what the radio broadcast. We carried on with the routine. When alarms were heard, we'd come out of work, on to the streets, prepared with our equipment.

I don't want to get political, but what a mistake Stalin made, a pact with Hitler to share Poland and Ukraine. Then Hitler reneged and attacked our beloved land our Ukraine. The earth is rich, fertile fields, forests a golden land. Underground coal and tin are mined. That is why it has always been attacked by Tartars, Mongols, Hungarians. Because the land is the wealthiest in the Soviet Union. No one could do anything when the foe stepped on to our land. When everything started to burn, sounds of bombs exploding, people in fright running away. I don't want anyone to see the cursed scenes I and my generation witnessed.

Poor Jewish people, I don't know why, from generation to generation they have suffered pogroms. Not only Jewish people suffered. In later years as a tourist when I travelled through Soviet Russia and Ukraine, every town had memorials to the war dead. Graves where 20,000 were buried next town 27,000. In every town war graves were seen everywhere I went, Leningrad (St Petersburg) but I'll tell you later.

Now everyday we started to see our heroes off. Our soldiers, pilots, nurses we were seeing them off with flowers and tears. Mothers crying, seeing their loved ones go to war, not knowing whether they'd meet again. We saw them off with tears, songs and flowers. They were going to defend the motherland, only for them to return a few days later wounded. The hospitals and schools were full with the casualties, some didn't return at all.

This now was our daily life, we weren't at the front but it was not far off. We were at the opposite side of the town from where the front line was, preparing to evacuate the town of Nikolayev. My husband came to me at my post to tell me the factory where he worked was being evacuated with its workers, and he had come to say goodbye. "Katya" he said "if we live we'll meet at your mother's place in the Donbas".

He was an orphan as I have said. His aunt brought him up, she loved me and used to say "Sasha, care for her she's an orphan same as you". I was so happy with him, even though I'd been raped, which left me with problems with physical contact. Believe me, with his love and gentleness, he helped me overcome a lot of my fear. I don't want to remember too much, because it hurts (in my heart).

Tearful as she recalls these memories.

Once, through the lanes and streets, the moon shone down on young women and men who strolled along, laughter in the air, music being played, a feeling of happiness. Maybe a plane was seen now and then as there was a military air base near the town, so planes were occasionally seen overhead. Now those streets saw troubled times, tears everywhere.

Every family had waved someone off to the front. Mothers with dread in their hearts, not knowing whether their loved ones were alive or fallen in battle. Everyday tens of thousands were returning wounded, no one knew what the future would bring, or what was waiting for us.

I was not frightened I was brave in fact I thought it was an honour to become a hero, defending the town. My job was to prepare documents for the evacuations. I had friends in different places, even in the NKVD (secret police).

Leaflets started to be dropped. The leaflets informed us of the cruelty that the Germans (Nazis) were inflicting on our people. The shooting and hanging of innocent civilians, fear was all around. It became very gloomy, streets started to be empty in the evening. People started to leave or preparing to leave. Some left to go to the villages where they thought they would be safer from the bombings there, than in town.

I stayed in Nikolayev to the last, in the government offices (Town Hall), there were only a few staff left, a couple of secretaries, few soldiers and militinairs (police). When I was on duty I had to make sure all the lights were turned off in the building before I made my way home to the edge of town, through darkened streets, and was never afraid that I would be attacked. Not like times are now (1990), afraid in your own home, that someone could break the door down and get in.

The days of war began with savageness.

The Germans (fascists, Nazi) were cruel, and brutal acts were seen throughout the Soviet Union lands. It's impossible even to think that such cruelty existed on this earth and humans could do such terrible things to other humans.

People started to evacuate, some decided to stay in denial as to the events, others didn't believe the Germans would harm them. Then there were the people who had nowhere to go or said "if we're going to get killed let it be in my own home."

We for the time being, stayed in beautiful Nikolayev, with its cleanliness, its greenery and gardens. As you walked in the town's streets, trees grew at the sides giving shade in the hot summer months. At the top end of the town was situated on Military Street a Cossack Soviet army base. Over the river was a college for sea cadets, and a small aerodrome, further down the river was a factory.

We were preparing and getting ready the wounded and the children, to send them to safety, doing nurses duties. Then came the order "retreat". The Germans had started to fire from the left side of the town, where the Town Hall was situated. They had approached with their tanks from the Besarabia or Moldovian side and had circled left of Nikolayev, we with the wounded (deep sign) had to retreat.

Convoys of vehicles were leaving the town, Red Cross trucks, lorries all different kinds of transport, taking the wounded, retreating, evacuating. We were with the children accompanying them, travelling through the lovely flat fields of Khersoncheni, which led us to the town of Kherson. We arrived at the river Dnipro, which runs through the town. On the banks was a cannery, where nearby there was a ferry crossing. The cannery was maybe 2 miles out of town.

Everywhere there was chaos, panic. It was bad here on this front, though it wasn't the front line. It was where the wounded and children arrived, hoping to be sent to safety. Evacuees all trying to get out of harms way, as far as they could get away, so they didn't fall into the hands of the Germans. The front line was somewhere near Nikolayev, re-enforcements had been sent from the Crimea. The battles on that front were savage. Sigh – that's as it was.

In the Kherson school, where we placed ourselves with the children, waiting the arrival of the wounded, were a large number of people. Teachers, town hall planners and officials, different people. It was full of evacuees, as the town of Kherson was the town everyone was heading for, away from the battle lines. Over those beautiful fields of Kherson flew the planes of the (zmeya) snakes, Nazi snakes, flying over those fields. Those planes appeared to us like eagles circling, hunting for prey near to the river and over the fields for they knew there was a crossing there on the river.

In tears recalling this memory.

One of the orders given to our group, was to help people get to the other side of the river. We had to remain till everyone had crossed; we were to be the last over. Bombs were being dropped so we tried to organise most of the crossings at night. One day a ferry full of children and wounded people was struck, most of the children drown, also the wounded. Lives came to an end on that day.

One morning, very early, just before dawn, bombs started to rain down on Kherson. That town, Kherson had lovely gardens and orchards that appeared to stretch for miles with their fruit trees of cherries, apple, pear and plum trees. Now they were broken, gardens downtrodden, ruined as people dashed to get to the river so no German would get them.

Early morning as the bombs fell, one exploded near our group, it was lucky that it fell into the ground as the soil flew at us and the earth covered and protected us. We had soil and debris in our mouths, up our noses, small shrapnel caught me. We were scratched from the debris, mouths and throats felt raw, as the planes started to fly away. People started to help each other and dug us out. We were dirty, soil in our mouths, noses, ears but it was good that we stayed alive. We got washed and tried to clean ourselves as best we could in the river Dnipro, and waited for our crossing, as we had an order to leave our post.

In all the mayhem and confusion our group split up, some had managed to get to the opposite bank, others were still waiting. A couple of us somehow got parted with our group. We were like lost sheep, **do what you will**, not knowing where or who to turn to. So much movement, everyone trying to get across the river as quick as possible. Vehicles of war, ambulances, children, people, mostly vehicles.

It was my good fortune that I got across to the other side of the river, because there I met our organiser from Nikolayev. He was a Jewish gentleman, an accountant. They had a lorry and it was full, packed tight with its human load, the accountant's mother, father, I think, other relatives, maybe friends. There was no one left, nobody to tag on to. I decided to make my way home to Donetsk. The journey that lay ahead was 330 miles.

As I was making my way home through the fields, not really knowing where I was heading, I met a small group and joined them. We walked and walked, no food just some bread in the bag. I don't know how far I'd walked, but I think it was all day. As evening approached a lorry stopped. "Where are you going Ekatarina Alexandrova?", "I don't know" I replied "I'm just walking, walking, walking". It was the accountant that I had attached (as in an official capacity) myself to. "Get in" he said. So I was lucky and got a lift to Donetsk.

Mama in tears

On our way as we reached Krivoy Rog we heard that there was savage fighting in Nikolayev. Soviet sailors were trying to defend the town, but the Germans had the upper hand and took Nikolayev. I met a man here in England who had been one of those sailors. He said that so many people had perished. The streets ran with blood, mixed with the water of broken drains and pipes.

I was still with a large group of people, the group had got larger, all different kinds of people, most had documents. My document (In the SU passports for identity also documents were carried) was made just before the war, in case of capture it said I came from the area/region of Astrakhan. In fact, I had quite a few documents on which I'd typed different information, name, surname, date of birth, place of birth etc, in case I had to escape the Nazis. They would be useful in going from one place to another.

We left Krivoy Rog travelling through the fields. We passed groups of people walking, livestock walking, bundles being carried with whatever possessions they could grab. Everyone fleeing the enemy to wherever they could, especially the Jewish people. From what I saw most of the Jews had transport, trucks, lorries, horse and carts, but in general people were walking. Wherever you looked people with their bundles were like flocks of sheep, all going ahead to the unknown.

Fortunately the weather was warm. Also the fields had not been harvested so potatoes were dug up and roasted, sweetcorn picked. Hunger was staved off for many with this gift from the fields.

In this way we arrived in Zaporizhya, breathing a sigh of relief, as we were further away from the front, and headed straight to the regional headquarters. There my bosses went to the warehouse and got food provisions, we drove on further to Dnipropetrovsk. Each town we came to the bosses had documents that allowed them provisions. My documents stated that I was going to Astrakan. I said to my chief the accountant, "When we get to Donetsk I want to go to my village to say goodbye to my mama". This was in August – I think the middle of August. I travelled by vehicle and walked.

The group I was with headed in another direction. I had to find someone to attach to. I got to Donetsk using any resources I could. I eventually arrived at my beloved familiar Chistakova (now Torez). After defending Nikolayev I had come so far, (maybe 370 miles as the crow flies) fleeing the Germans. I could not stay at my post, as the orders were given. We had to leave with the children and wounded. When we had fulfilled our duty everyone dispersed, going their own way. Maybe the tragedy which occurred of which I'm going to tell would not have happened if I had gone straight to Astrakan in the Urals.

My husband was already at our village, he had been wounded during a bombing raid. He couldn't be sent to the front, so volunteered to go to our area and was sent to work as a driver. All these events took place before my arrival at Chistakova.

When my husband Shura, arrived at my parents home, he told them the last he had seen of me was in Nichalaev, where I had stayed to help defend the town against the fascists. When my mother and father heard this they were distraught. Then the news reached the village that Nikolayev had been taken by the enemy. They were filled with grief; they thought I had been taken prisoner, or even worse, dead! But I was alive! Striving to get to my beloved Chistakova. I would have got there quicker, but it wasn't in my power.

We lived near to the train station. It was a main station. Every evening an express trained passed through. Every evening my husband and mother went to the station to greet this train, it was named Zhilavajska to Dibaltovo on its way to another main station. Like all the other mothers, fathers, relatives they were asking the same questions of passers by. "Have you seen?", "Have your heard?", "Have you seen anything of …?" "Do you know …..?" All wondering, hoping to hear news of their loved ones.

Leaflets were thrown from the passing trains with news of German atrocities. The shooting of comsomolties (young communist league) and Jewish people. Some were doubtful about the leaflets, saying "Oh! They wouldn't do that, they didn't do that in the First World War." Others though thought, as my father thought, he used to say "Oh no! Never, the Germans won't get here."

I had written to my family from Zaparozh, to let them know I was alive and trying to make my way home as soon as possible. This changed their disquiet to relief. Now every day they would go to the station to see if I was on any of the trains. One evening I was getting off a train (I've forgotten which train) as I alighted I saw my husband running towards me, arms wide open, smiling. He grabbed hold of me hugging and kissing me, my mother behind him crying, sobbing with relief and joy. I recall my father was there with my young brothers and sister.

I stayed in Chistakova, organisations were in turmoil anyway. I was given a position at the Town Hall with the (NKS). It was nice being at home with my mother and family, but day by day we didn't know what to expect or what to do. Again orders were given to evacuate. "Oh the Germans won't come here" my father kept repeating. Many people stayed, for like me and my friends, they also didn't believe the enemy would reach us.

Life went on as normal with us waiting for our instructions. Then everything started to be destroyed, by our side, buildings burnt, fields set on fire. The word had come that the fascists were getting nearer and not to let anything get into their hands. My husband and I were given orders to retreat. I had been home about a month. We started to get ready for retreat.

Chapter Eight

OCTOBER 1941

The weather was pleasant that evening, somewhere in the distance bombs were being dropped, explosions heard above our heads, the sound of aeroplanes as they flew overhead.

Then began the most, the most terrible, terrible, terrifying night at my home, in my village, at our train station. Sigh!

On this evening we were at home, father, mother, grandma who was living out her last years with us, my brothers and sister and my cousin Halya, who was the daughter of gran's sister and had gone to gran's. Her mum had died and the father wanted her to be like a "wife", so she came to us to escape him.

Outside people were going about their business, or sat in small groups, some were afraid, others not afraid. One man's voice could be heard saying "If the Germans come here I'll shoot them all!" Other voices replied "our lads are beating them back," or "they won't get here, they're on the retreat."

To tell the truth, it had gone quieter near us, we didn't know or see anything. The front line had gone downwards away from us into the valley. We didn't know or see anything. My mama had started baking bread, with dough she had prepared earlier in the panshan. When the loaves were taken out of the oven they had truly risen and the smell of the baked bread was lovely. Gran looked at the loaf saying "aah, we might not get the chance to eat them. It was like this for me in 1914. I had prepared the dough, ready to start baking when we had to flee and with my children had to wander into the unknown."

"Oh Gran" I replied, "don't say that." We joked and the conversations were light hearted. My cousin who was very shy was joking with my husband, as he always used to tease her. It all appeared peaceful and we all laid down to sleep.

Family group who were at home when the house was bombed.

Left to right top row – Valya, Grandad Grigory, Great Grandma Paraska, Mama Katya.

Bottom left to right – Vitya, Mitya, Grandma Anna and Sasha.

Though the house appeared large to mama (Katya), it was a small cottage, so the sleeping arrangements would have been really tight, but that was no problem, as this was before the days of having a bed to yourself, – never mind a room.

In the middle of the night we were awoken by a loud explosion and gunfire. My father had just said that we should go to the underground cellar we had in the garden under the shed, which was accessed by a trapdoor. All village houses had these cellars, which were dug out mostly in the garden. In some homes they were dug in the kitchen. They were used to store food as it was very cool. They were accessed by a trapdoor.

If we had gone out then together, we would had been mown down as one, with only pieces of flesh left of us. The bomb missed the tanks and hit our shed. When it hit our shed, debris and splinters blasted out with the power of the explosion. Gardens and our orchard mown down, our house damaged.

Just prior to the explosion my mother went into the kitchen, followed by my father and husband. She opened the door to go into the yard, at the same moment, as I remember. I opened a door inside to enter into the kitchen, and the world appeared to explode.

Mama (Katya) – only recently I have been told, when I visited my family it wasn't a Nazi bomb as I thought. It was one of our own Soviet bombs. Apparently not far from our house the Germans had entered with their tanks. The Soviet pilot had seen the tanks and had dropped a bomb.

Until my mama Katya heard this we were always told, and we believed that the Germans had bombed, because they had seen a light as the door was opened.

The door fell on top of me, my heel was ripped off. My cousin who was only 16, beautiful Halya, a tall girl with lovely thick hair that she wore in plaits. A splinter had hit her, and ripped her stomach apart. I remember my little brother had a splinter in his leg. I must have passed out, because I remember as I came round, there was the horrid smell of paraffin, which had been stood in the hall. It had fallen over and had got soaked up with a sack of flour which had also been stored there in the corridor.

I'm holding my emotions, my tears, so that I can tell you clearly the events we lived through in that war. That's why I will always stand for peace.

As mama Katya was telling this she was in tears. Very distraught with the memories that she was recalling.

It was fortunate the paraffin had not set alight, or we would have all been burned to cinders. My cousin Halya, was crying, pleading, "Katya, Katya," she wailed. It was 29 October. "Katya, Katya, she cried". I crawled towards her, not realising that my heel was hanging off, trailing behind me. As I reached her, I put my hands on her stomach. Her intestines (guts) were spilling out. I went numb. "Katya, help me", "Katya help me". I tried pushing her guts back into her stomach, and I passed out.

I came round, everything was hazy. Hearing my little brother crying. My mama shouting, grandma pleading for help. Children (brothers and sister), shouting and crying, and that horrible smell appeared to be everywhere.

I don't know how many times I lost consciousness. It was dark, it was night. I dragged myself along the ground, leaving my cousin, knowing that I couldn't do anything for her.

My mother was calling out and I headed in her direction. She was laying in the yard. "Mama, where's my Shura?" I asked. "Here, here" she answered. "Mama, where's Dad?" "Here, here," she said. "How are you?" I asked. "Help me" she whispered. I started screaming, shouting. "People, good people, help us. Please someone help".

No one, not one person, came to our rescue. Everyone had taken refuge. Hidden away, afraid of the dropping bombs exploding all around us. With their children, families were seeking safety in their underground rooms. Because here the enemy was death. Flying round our houses, hovering over our gardens.

I crawled back to Halya. "Halya, Halya" I cried. She didn't answer, poor thing. She had been pushing herself along the floor on her back; I thought that she was dead. She died, just before daybreak. No one could have saved her. The stomach had been badly damaged. Now she was out of her pain.

"Mama, mama," I wept. "Help me, oh help me" she replied. "They're laid here under me where I am". Heads had been decapitated, limbs severed, only flesh left. I, my little sister Valya, and young brothers tried to get the debris off them, clawing with our hands. We pulled my mama out of the rubble. She was weeping. My poor dear Mama was covered in blood.

My uncle and neighbours came running up. I remember they brought light, a lantern. We saw my mama covered in blood, wounds all over her. Neighbours carried her to my uncle's house. My small brothers aged 2 years, 5 years and 9 years, and my sister Valya aged 11 years remained in the ruins of our home. To be taken care of by my gran.

War is cruel, cruel. People! People! In such a tragic moment. They had come from who knows where to loot places that had been bombed. Our grain and hay were stolen. Chickens, geese, or whatever they could catch they took. One man was rummaging around in our garden. When asked "what are you searching for." "Ah" he answered, "everyone here has been killed, so they have no need of anything." I was left alone.

I remember after my mama had been carried away, I crawled further into our yard. Everywhere stank. Buzzing, droning noise everywhere. The bombings continued. Not far from our house, a bomb fell, killing 5 people in their house as it was raised to the ground. Further down the road, more human lives taken. My uncle's house was damaged but no one was hurt or killed.

Though the Front was down below us in the valley, these events took place in West Chistakova (Torez). At the top, where amongst others, our house was situated.

When I realised that my dad, and my husband Shura had been killed, I got a feeling that I did not want to live. Because I had been raped, I always felt afraid. My darling husband, because he loved me so much, had taught me to live life.

I wondered what the burning sensation was. I crawled into the yard. It was a moonlit night. No – now I remember, a drizzle starting later. Then I looked at my foot, where the burning sensation was because my heel was hanging off. I put my heel back in place and wrapped it in a rag. "Ah!" I sighed, if there is a God. I didn't believe in God and used to make fun of my gran and grandad and their belief in God. They were very religious, had icons that they revered. I was young, a patriot, and religions was opium for poor people.

Events that occurred in my life changed my view. There is a power somewhere. I don't believe in pomp, ceremony or regalia, but a power that gave me the stubbornness, heroism, if you like, **not** to give in, **not** to give in, **not** to give in. No matter how many times my legs were knocked from under me, I rose. Though at times it was difficult, I did not give in.

I knelt on my knees in the yard. Thoughts of my leg been amputated filled me with dread. I looked up to the skies and started praying. "God"

I shouted. "If there is a God, what God are you? Are you Maria, St Peter, Paul, Jesus? God who are you?" "I don't want to be a war wounded" I shouted. "A cripple." I started shouting, screaming. "Kill me, kill me." Over and over I screamed. "Kill me, I don't want to live."

Then it appeared to me that I was stood on a black canvas that covered all the earth. Straight and even, wherever the eyes looked, they saw a black canvas stretched before them, and at the same time there was a twinkle in the sky, like, or maybe a star. Into my heart came the emotion of defiance.

I wept, as I said to myself, don't submit, you have brothers and sisters, don't yield. You still have your mother, be strong. You are a sister, be strong. With those thoughts my feelings changed. Now I didn't ask God to kill me, I asked for his help. Help me for the sake of my brothers and sister I wept. Help me for the sake of my mother, their mother who was wounded and fortunate that she survived.

My poor unfortunate brothers and sister, they were so young and didn't understand what was happening, they were only children. My poor babooshka (gran), she was old, running around. Half out of her mind, not knowing what to do. I crawled out dragging my leg that I'd wrapped, I was so alone, and I just sat outside all night.

I was still sitting in the same spot when the Front started to pass. German soldiers were at the front. The Italians and Rumanians followed next. The tanks rumbled by. At the rear, Germans again. I shouted "shisen! shisen! shisen!", "shoot me, shoot me, shoot me." I'd looked at my leg it was covered in blood, heavy I couldn't lift it. The horror of being a cripple, suffering, filled me with dread. Again I was asking for death, but they hurried by me, the Front was passing.

They, the soldiers, were also like frightened mice, scuttling forward. Stooping, darting, glances backwards, the tanks rumbling. They were in a foreign land, and not one of them knew whether he'd return. He wasn't to blame that he was there. They were sent – ordered. As I saw The Rumanians and Italians were between the Germans. Germans soldiers at the front, German tanks at the rear and behind the tanks another German unit, pushing them forward and behind.

I'm against any regime that wants war. The unfortunate nations, the soldiers, the poor civilians, they don't want war. Not one mother want to see her son go into battle. I wouldn't want my son or grandson to go to war. As now, in different parts of our planet, conflicts are still raging, but it's not in our power. It's in the hands of millionaires, those that want to become even wealthier. For some people, war brings untold wealth. Millions, billions for them and their descendants.

The less fortunate of a nation have to suffer, they can't get onto a plane and flee to safety. To the USA or have bunkers built in case there is an atomic war so he can try and protect him and his. Unfortunate ones have to wait for whatever will be. If ever some mad ruler presses that red button, the earth will be torn apart and it is the poor innocent children that will suffer. These war games that are played out in this world of ours is not in my, or your, power to stop. I know my words won't reach far, or be printed in a book, but I've given you my thoughts in word.

The strange life began. Again the misfortune, again suffering. Death flying round like a bird, an eagle hunting his prey. The retreating populous were afraid, many cold and hungry. In our area named Stantia (station). The place was called Station because of the railway station nearby. In Stantia we had food, potatoes and other produce. It was autumn so the harvest had been gathered. The refugees had left everything in their haste to retreat. Only a few meagre possessions they had grabbed, and their children by their sides hungry. Some of our villagers gave them what food they could spare, others had nothing to give. Everything they had, had been destroyed or stolen. What could they do? That's war!

Well again my life begins.

I'm sat on the street, on my own, like an old woman (beggar). Once more praying, asking God for his help. Along comes a local neighbour, passing by with his family. With him he had his horse and cart. "Dyadya (uncle) take me with you", I said. "I don't want to sit here, the house has been damaged." (Uncle – a term of respect used when addressing older people).

At the self same time some people had started digging a hole in our garden. My Shura's (husband) pieces were gathered, my cousin Halya's body, and my dad's remains. All placed in the same pit, buried, but at peace in the garden. I never saw them, but they were buried under a cherry tree that is still there. My mama was at my uncles and my gran was looking after the children in what was left of our home.

People can be cruel. Some came to steal what they could. Gran tried defending, tried to keep them away the best she could. Produce, possessions couldn't be placed where it was secure as everything was in ruins. Some neighbours came, got some planks of wood that were strewn about, nailing them to the house, so there was some kind of shelter.

The cart stopped. "Uncle" I said, "Take me with you." (The word "uncle or aunt" tended to be used instead of Mr or Mrs). They took me with them, placing me on the cart with the wounded leg still wrapped in its blooded rag. I was wearing a coat and headscarf. It was chilly. We all went onwards heading for the coalmine. We rode over the fields, reaching the river where we were going to cross.

The river, our river, where once we enjoyed our lives on its banks. Entertained by music, as we strolled or danced to its sounds. We used to catch fish in our river and children played, paddled, bathed. Treats for ice cream were for sale, when I was younger by this river. Now this river will flow with hot blood and burning fear flies overhead. People feel dread, they don't know what awaits them, or what events will unfold.

We cross the river, eventually reaching the mine. It was a drift mine, not long open. (Drift mine, no shaft but an entrance that descends underground). At the entrance there was some straw. My companions placed me on the straw, it was nice and warm there, and a feeling of safety crept over me. Oh! I thought, bombs won't reach me, grenades won't reach me, nothing will.

My companions headed down the steps that led underground into the mine. Other families went down there with their lamps. Husbands with the wives and children. Elderly descending to hide in the mine.

I lay there not far from the entrance. Can anyone understand the emotion of being completely alone. After all the events I lost my child. I was a couple of months pregnant; I lay on that straw bleeding.

Later I looked and saw figures moving in the entrance. It looked like children walking forward. It was my Valya, my sister 11 years of age; she was carrying 2 year old Vitya in her arms. Mitya, 9 was holding 4 year old Sasha by his hand. As they walked they were chatting. They were going into the mine to hide. I recognised my little brothers and sister's voices. "Whose there" I called. "Valya is it you I can hear, where are you going." "Yes Katya" she replied. "We're going into the mines to hide from the Germans, we're afraid of them."

"Sit by me" I wept. "My darling children, my little ones, don't go anywhere you might get lost" I sobbed. They came up to me and sat down. Bombs started dropping again. I put my arms around them. After a while it went quiet. The bombing appeared to have subsided. I looked at them "Go, go to our uncle's where mama is laying wounded in the cellar. Go don't leave her, don't leave her side, don't go anywhere. The Germans/Italians could beat you, rape you. The soldiers could kill you" I wept. They left.

As I watched them walk away I was distraught. Crying praying that they would arrive safe back to mama. Sometime later folk returning to the Stantia village said that they had seen them west of Chistakova heading to our uncle's house where mama lay.

I lay there on that straw alone and hungry, feeling hot from a high temperature that I'd developed. I started to doze then dropped asleep. As dusk was falling I felt someone trying to wake me. I looked up it was Alexandrovna, a teacher in mathematics who had taught me when I was a young schoolgirl. "Who is it" she asked. "Katya Alexandrovna" I answered. "Katya" she gasped. "What are you doing here?" Neighbours brought me here, I'm wounded and can't walk anywhere" tearfully I said. "I don't know what to do or where to go, there's no one who can take me anywhere".

She returned back home with her son and came back with a wheelbarrow. Lifting me into the barrow they told me that they were taking me to the hospital. As we made our way to the hospital, 2 planes started a dogfight over our heads. On our arrival at the hospital we found just one nursing sister. All the staff had gone. A veterinary surgeon was there trying to attend to the injured. All round lay casualties, some were dying, others who could not be saved dead, some unfortunates had been shot by the Germans, their corpses lay on a pile of straw.

I crawled along the floor looking for some aid. There was no one who could help me; there was no one, apart from the Germans, the wounded, the dying and the dead. The Doctors had fled, or maybe been killed.

During the recounting of these episodes mama/grandma Katya is distraught, though the events took place such a long time ago in late 1941 also recalling –

Sigh- How difficult it is to recollect this, I'd lost a child, I was only 2 no 3 months pregnant. Blood had been running out of me for 2 days. When I was taken to hospital my womb/insides were cleaned. No anaesthetic. I was tied to a bed, held down while the procedure was carried out.

It was such a horrible thing I did not want to recall it, but I must, I must tell of my pain.

The miscarriage. It was dreadful! My husband was so happy I was with child. He would have carried me in his arms. He was so gentle with me rejoicing that I was pregnant.

Eventually the vet and nurse cleaned me up and bandaged my foot. "Will I be able to walk" I enquired. "Yes he answered, "but we have no medicines." He had given me first aid, and in a couple of days the pain had eased. Everyone left, I remained in the hospital. I dragged myself across the floor. Bodies of injured souls, bodies of the dying, bodies that were lifeless.

As evening fell I crawled out of the hospital towards the gates. I managed to get to the street side of the entrance and sat there outside in the dark and cold. An icy drizzle had just started to fall. It was dark, it was frightening as I sat there by those gates. I started to invoke God, praying to him. God help me, I pleaded, God help me. As I called out to the powers above, I saw someone was running past. "Auntie" (Mrs) I called out. "Who is it" I asked. She approached me. "What are you doing here" she uttered. I've been in this hospital" I replied. There's no one there but the dead and the dying. A vet has attended to me and bandaged my foot. I've dragged myself out, I could not stay in there in the dark, and it stinks." She left to fetch her husband.

It was forbidden to be out of doors after sundown or you'd be shot. No one had the right to be out after dark. The lady arrived back with her husband supporting me under my arms; they took me back to their home. Somehow help always appeared to arrive. It was a house that belonged to the coal mine (shahta) 8-9, where workers that were employed in the mines were housed.

I remember they gave me a biscuit cracker. They didn't have much that belonged to them, but they gave me something to eat and a place to sleep. I stayed there a couple of days with that poor young couple. Then conveyed a message to my uncle telling him where I was.

My uncle got angry. "She's got a small scratch" he raged "and hidden herself away just so that she doesn't have to do anything." I wept when I heard what he had said. I remained in that tiny house. Eventually someone brought me provisions from home. Flour etc. I cannot recall who was sent to bring me food, Valya maybe. The vet used to come to clean and redress my wound. After staying with that young couple a little longer I knew it was time to leave. They didn't have the space or the food. They had helped me in my hour of need, now was the time to return home.

Chapter Nine

SAVING THE PIG

My uncle hired some transport and came to collect me. On his arrival he scolded me saying I'd hidden myself away so I didn't have to do anything. "Uncle, I couldn't do anything, my foot is injured", I tried to explain. That was my plight; ill, wounded, my mama injured, everything in ruins. I was brought back home.

Germans, Italians tearing about, looting everything. Dragging inhabitants out of their homes. A particular focus was on the Jewish people and comsomol (communist youth). They were taken away.

Not far from where we lived in Chistakova, there was a square. My aunt Maryoosya, my mother's sister, went to spend a couple of days with an acquaintance whose home was there. On her return she told us of the events she had witnessed. "There's such fearful goings on", she said. She told us every evening, large lorries arrived at the square, we were told to close our shutters, but through a small hole in the wooden shutters we peeped. The lorries were unloaded of their human cargo, women children. There on that square, they were executed. Poor Aunt Maryoosya was so upset with the scene.

Soldiers were looting from the villagers' homes, taking everything they could. I was looking after my wounded mama; my leg was painful and terribly swollen. I couldn't bear the burning pain in my leg, I was so ill.

When the sound of planes were heard, I hid my little brothers and sister. Pushing them under the bed, laying on the outside of them, trying to squeeze them further under, so my body would protect them, as if I was a door. The thoughts running through my head were, my body will protect them, if I get killed they will survive.

When I visited home recently (1980?), my sister Valya said she remembered those days, my brother Vitya also remembered.

Well, such a life began.

Winter arrived, with it the cold. Children young, poor gran and Valenka (Valya) tried to run the household with my brother Mitya trying to be the "man" of the house. He was only 8/9 years of age; he was such a good little lad.

My leg had got worse. All night I'd been awake crying with the pain of it. One morning I was sat changing the dressings on my mama's wounds, washing her injuries, also my own. I'd open the dressing and cleaned it using salt water as we had no medicines. The next morning my friend Vyera came, she looked at my leg, then left. (Vyera was my friend with whom I was in the German Labour Camps. After the war she returned back home to the Ukraine).

I was attending to my mama, who was seated near the window. As I glanced through the window I saw a large man walking towards our house, flanked by 2 German soldiers. My heart started to race with fear, but he had come to my aid. Vyera had been to a German hospital to beg them for someone to help me. An army doctor! That's who the big man was! My aunt and sister told me what occurred as I didn't remember anything of the following events.

He looked at my foot and told them to heat some water and flake soap into it. The water had to be as hot as I could bear. The 2 soldiers picked me up, placing my leg in the water up to my knee. Although the water was warm, it felt as if my foot was being scolded. I shouted out loudly, then passed out. When I was raised out of the soapy liquid, I was told my wound was so ghastly, only raw red flesh could be seen. Then my foot was bandaged. The German army doctor came to our place occasionally, God bless him he was in my prayers for his kindness. Neighbours would collect eggs, milk, whatever they could spare to give him, for him to take to the hospital.

After the first onslaught of battle the circumstances changed. German troops were quartered in local homes, no choice was given, refusal was out of the question. No one was billeted with us, but my uncle had a military man staying in his house. The soldiers were wary of us. Daytime they were seen in the locality, but when night fell they kept out of sight, for fear of being encircled and trapped by the partisans, which had happened on occasions.

What can I say; the regular German soldiers did not beat us. They were more concerned with fighting at the front, which was now 5 miles ahead; then getting back to their rooms to rest before heading back to do battle. The real problems started when the corrective unit (Gestapo) arrived. They were callous with their methods, shooting etc.

Our local police (Ukrainian) were also a problem. They were so pompous, proud that they had been given some power, which was represented by a club and a badge that they wore. These symbols gave them the authority to take whatever took their fancy. A coat, a pair of boots, if their demands were not met, or if they had a previous grudge against anyone, it could easily be arranged to have whoever had crossed them handed in to the enemy.

It was just after Christmas, snow covered the ground. I was starting to hobble around on my homemade crutches, my foot had started to improve, thank the Lord! As I gazed through our window, I saw a vehicle drive into our yard. There were 2 figures inside, one was one of our local police (Ukrainian), the other one was a German, a fat man.

I can visualise the events as if it had just happened. What I am telling is like a record playing in my head; no lies. Over the years I've repeated those incidents to many people. I could not forget it; from start to finish I couldn't forget it, because I carried the past with me. Always in my mind, in my feelings – forever telling it so it could not be forgotten. Events such as these are never forgotten. It stays with you in your head till death, now back to my story.

As I watched, they drove through our garden and stopped by our shed. Turning to my gran I asked, "What are they going there for?" "They're going for the pig", my gran answered, for we still had a pig. Picking up my crutches I went outside and started approaching them on my crutches in the snow. When they got out of the vehicle I was standing by the shed. "Why have you come here?" I asked. "What do you want?" "We have come for your pig, our orders! We've heard you've got a pig!" I screeched, (I have a strong voice) and I kept on shouting and screeching. Local folk started to run to our place to see what the commotion was about. A crowd had gathered in our garden, (if only I had a picture of the scene).

I'm stood by the shed trying to beat them off with my crutches, they were not armed, only the club of our local policeman, with which he tried to hit me, but each time he tried to get near me, I raised my crutch to beat him off.

The crowd started to raise their voices, baying "you bastard! you swine! see 3 corpses are buried there, they pointed to the spot, "there!" other voices were heard. "Look! look at the young children." My pitiable brother and sister were stood looking through the window, no trousers on, almost naked as they gazed at us.

My gran came up to me taking me by the arm, she tried pulling me crying, "For God's sake, come away, let them take the pig." "No! I shouted, "Over my dead body! That's the only way this pig will be taken, no! The Germans have taken enough, stolen everything." I continued my tirade. "They've taken my dad! taken my husband, taken everything!, our house is in ruins, everything gone, I am not giving them the pig!" As I shouted this I was adamant.

Two or three dozen people had gathered by then so the local policeman and German soldier turned to leave reluctantly, but I was on their "marked list". (So maybe it was fortunate that they took me to forced Labour Camps, as no doubt at some point I would have been taken and shot).

The German soldier was trying to persuade our "man" to come away, edgy about the crowd who had gathered in our garden, but the local policeman was still trying to get the pig. Eventually they left. My eldest brother Mitya knew the local man, but didn't know what happened to him.

On many occasions "our police" paid our home a visit, banging their clubs on the floor to see if we had anything below (underground cellar). I asked them angrily "What are you looking for in here? Go and look in the garden, there! You will find 3 corpses under the ground! That's what you will find! What are you searching in here for?"

Mama was in tears recalling. You know it was a difficult, difficult life, difficult for most of the people caught in that awful conflict.

Later my leg was easier, even though at times after all these years (over 50 years ago?) it still at times gives me pain. They wanted to operate on my foot here in England, as a nerve had been severed, that was what caused the problem. I was always on my feet when the children were small. Lots to do (no washer, no cooker, cooking was all done on a Yorkshire range, no hot water). The doctor told me when I was on my feet a lot, it disturbed my nervous system, I used to scream and shout at my children.

In tears recalling.

Time passed, spring was not far in the distance. We had coal, also wood, as fuel for the fire which my Tato (Ukrainian for dad) had stock piled for the winter before he was so cruelly taken from us.

My poor little brother, Mitochka (Mitya), he now at the age of 8/9? years was "master" of the house. He would bring the coal from outdoors into the house, trying to keep us warm, clear the snow. Little Valya also helped him with the "man's work." Also we had good neighbours who helped us.

Those poor, sad little ones. One cold morning, a few weeks after Christmas, I happened to look through the window, and noticed my young brother Mitya, going somewhere. All he was wearing was a shirt and trousers, a pair of boots on his feet, far too large for him. Where's he going? I thought as I watched. He went into my dad's workshop.

The workshop contained all the tools anyone would need, as dad was a skilled craftsman in many things. Some time passed: as I glanced through the window I saw him dragging a wooden cross across the snow to the mound in our garden.

I called to gran "come and look what Mitya is doing." He had nailed together some wood to make a cross using all his small body's strength, he erected the cross securely on the grave. Imagine what it was like!

Katya's brother years later was to become a teacher and artist. Him and his wife Shura had one son who was killed in a mining accident leaving them with one grandson. Mitya died of Parkinsons Disease sometime in the 1990's.

Mama laid wounded helpless, kiddies small, house almost in ruins and in the garden a cross dug into a mound, under which was my beloved husband, dad and cousin where their remains had been placed.

Chapter Ten

Start of Transportation

Continuous bombings as one squadron flew away, another squadron appeared. Day after day the mayhem, the turmoil, tanks coming and going, to and fro from the front line which had moved ahead, but was not far away from us.

My girlfriends paid me a visit to suggest that we all retreat. This was about March/April. I should have retreated earlier and not listened to my Dad saying, "Oh the Germans won't come here", then maybe there would have been a chance of being classed as a hero on home soil; but I'm now on foreign soil as if I am an enemy to my homeland. How could I retreat or cross to any safety on crutches on a painful leg, therefore we stayed.

Life carried on one way or another. Many of the populous arrested, many taken away, shot. Then an order was issued. All individuals of a certain age, and able to work had to go to Germany. If you went voluntarily then your family that was left behind would be issued with rations. There was one German who helped our people when he could, I have forgotten his name. This German came to our house one evening to give us some advice. I could communicate, as I spoke, wrote and read German pretty well, as I had been taught German at school. His advice was this:

"If you go to Germany voluntarily your mama, brothers and sister will receive rations, don't be obstinate or you will be taken by force. If you try and run or hide all the same you will be found and maybe shot. It's better to go quietly then your family will be supported". We had to go. I was not obstinate, nor did I try and run away or hide. There was no where to run or hide, so we had no choice. (Explanation of Labour camps Glossary) I was to find out later that any young Komsomol or youth that had been rebellious (my name had been taken because of the incident with the pig so I was on this list) were taken and executed and my mother would have witnessed my death. I escaped execution by being taken as forced labour. I had to leave my wounded mama, my brothers and sister, my gran, everything I cherished and held dear I had to leave behind and go to a foreign land. I had no choice but to go to a foreign land for more torment, but I came through everything. I had to tell what I lived through. It's so very, very important that my grandchildren and great grandchildren know this history.

One day, I and my friends, Maria, Vyera, Valya, Tonya and Halya gathered some belongings. We were preparing to make our way to the Town Hall where we had to assemble. I gathered some rations of sala, salami and bread. I put on the dress that my mama had sewn for me, my blouse that mama had embroidered, my heavy boots and a large shawl so that I was dressed warm. Mothers and relatives were distraught. Weeping families gathered to see us leave. So much misery, some of the girls were only 16 years of age. In fact Halya and Tanya were only 16, I think. Halya and Tanya returned after the war and married. As for me, I don't remember who came to see me off. I had one thought going through my head – I have to go, I have to go, to help my mama, brothers and sister so they would not die of hunger.

Our journey (madrivka) began.

They marched us off towards Makeyavka? a town. We trudged in the snow for hours, being herded along like a flock of sheep, over the fields we trekked. Not as before when we were retreating from Kherson, then it was warm as it was late summer, now it was the end of winter, cold, snow still covered the ground. In this snow on this long road we tramped, towards torment and labour and German camps.

We arrived in Makayavka where we were loaded into lorries and then we were driven to Stalinov (Donetsk) Railway station. No! – maybe Makeavka station. I can't say for certain which station it was, but I do remember how long the train was. With wagons that had small windows with wire netting over them, and straw strewn on the floor. The procedure began of loading us into the wagons.

The German soldiers were trying to speed us up shouting "Schnell! Schnell! Rouse! Rouse! But **our heros, our police** were stood with clubs. If someone was not fast enough, or looked at them the wrong way, would beat or prod you with his club. I watched these acts of spite, but kept silent because I was afraid.

I won't be as distraught as before, so will be able to speak more coherently until I get to the harsh conditions again in prison and concentration camps.

Our departure was on a spring day. No! it was April or March I think as snow still laid on the ground. It's difficult to remember everything, as 46 years have past.

We were loaded onto the wagons; I'm not sure whether it was Makeavka or Stalinov (Donetsk). As I have stated previously, our police were very arrogant. They were fed on German food and had privileges. They were given the right to beat us, instead of trying to help their countrymen/women, they were proud of the position they held. In some cases taking revenge on slights they perceived real or imagined.

We were loaded into the straw carpeted wagons. Many of this human cargo were packed in, 40 maybe more. Various ages of men, women, teenage boys and girls. Everyone that was capable to work. Many were from Chistakova (Torez) some I knew well. With me was Maria Shootakova, Tanya, Halya, another Maria whose surname I have forgotten, Lida and other girls. Also of course there were inhabitants of other towns and villages. From Volhovchik there was Misha of whom you'll hear about later, his uncle and cousin.

The journey to Germany began. Inside the wagon there was no toilet facility of any description. No bucket, no container, nothing. When it was really necessary to urinate, or want a number 2, dignity had to be forgotten. Crouching in the corner in the straw was the only thing to be done. The stink waftered through the wagon, it couldn't be evaded. It was as if we were livestock.

We had no choice, we had to resign ourselves to our fate, accept what was happening. For no one wants to die, but fights anyway he can to survive, endures anything to live while ever he/she has the strength.

We sat on the floor, chatting, discussing events; the air was foul, sickening. The small wired window was open slightly. It was cold, but never mind we huddled up to one another trying to keep warm, and in this way we would doze, sat propped up, with one another's bodies.

We travelled many, many hours. Here and there the train stopped. At these pull ups we were herded into the fresh air as if we were cattle. It was difficult to get out, as the wagons had no steps. No means of getting off as it was rather a high drop to get to the ground, we had to help one another scramble down, or jump. Misha appeared to be always there to help to assist and help me down safely.

As the "passengers" got off, everyone made their way to the fields to do their toilet business. A mass all crouching, averting their eyes from one another, to try to hide their shame and embarrassment. The Germans just observed us because to them it was livestock they were transporting not human beings. Herded back onto the wagons the journey continued.

It was possible to pull yourself up, or if someone lifted you, to look through the wired window, onto the outside world. There in the fields bodies were seen, laid here and there. It was said that when we had our stops some of the "passengers" tried to run to escape. They were shot. Their journey ended in some unknown field. Trying to forget our fear and forget what we had seen, to put it in the past, we continued our journey to Germany.

One stop was at a place called Kovel. That was a time when I witnessed a group of people clearing snow. It was the first time I saw the star sown on their backs so everyone would know that they were Jewish people. They uttered not one word to us. We saw prisoners, more transport trains, screaming shouting, police shooting and you didn't know if it was your turn next. Some Poles, oh! I don't know who they were! mocked us, jeering "you do know where you're going?" No – we didn't know where we were going, we were going to wherever we were taken to make us into dog food or whatever else. We didn't know what our journey's end would be.

As we travelled on Misha was taken ill. I had a little medical knowledge, from my days in the nursing unit. I, Maria and Tanya nursed him, putting compresses on his brow, trying to feed him as we had bread and a little food. He was very ill, but gradually began to improve. We tried to protect him the best we could.

At one of our stops Misha had a close shave. As the wagons rumbled to a halt a German soldier looked into our "carriage", noticing Misha laid down started to enquire what was wrong. We were afraid to say that he was ill. We propped him up, supporting him to make everything look as if it was normal. The soldier walked away. Misha could have been shot, or if he had died would have been thrown off the moving train.

Hours, days past. Time had lost its meaning. The atmosphere was gloomy. With heavy hearts we travelled, travelled, travelled, day and night in that putrid, stinking air. It felt as if we were never going to reach our destination. Sometimes a train would stop at a station. The wagons could be stood, half a day, or a full day, and then we would chug away again. In this way we clanked on our way to Germany. When we stopped we were given water, or some soup, I don't remember which. I know it was a gruelling journey. After maybe a week when we arrived at Cologne we were ravenous.

So this was our journey's end. It was a beautiful place by the river Rhine. A bridge was situated there, nearby was a cathedral. Not far from the cathedral were some buildings that appeared to be garages. We were herded into these premises where again there was the straw, covering the floor. There, thousands of us were crowded in, 4000 transportees who had arrived on our train.

We remained there, sitting around for a couple of days. On the third day we had visitors, some of the citizens of Cologne came, landowners, farmers, factory owners etc, Gestapo and police were also present. These arrogant "masters" with their gentlemen's hats and sticks had come to pick out their workforce. Poking and prodding as if we were animals and they were traders dealing in livestock.

First males were arranged in a column. The future "masters" passed by, choosing which male he wanted for his workforce. I tell no lie; they examined their choice by looking into their mouths at their teeth, feeling their muscles, prodding their preference with a stick. They were then taken out of the queue. I sat in a corner watching the circus with a bleeding heart. When will it be your turn? Where will you be going and what will be waiting for you?

Then the females joined the column, the younger ones were the first, followed by the older women. We in our group kept hiding, making our way to the back of the line. Families stayed together, relatives, people who had known one another back in their home towns tried to be with each other. Lads and lasses who'd got acquainted with each other as they were being transported went off together as husband and wife.

Thousands did this, then after the war they were ashamed to admit they weren't legally married. Others would just go to the authorities and say we weren't married we just got together. They parted, that was it no divorce needed. Many documents were burnt after the war so there was no evidence. Many couples whom after the war fled to safety in the West, Britain, USA, Canada etc kept their secret.

Finally there was only our group left; we were to go to work in a factory. Misha came up to me and quietly said, "Katya, can we stay together as brother and sister?", "No! I don't want to" I replied. "Please, it will be easier for us", he said "No!" I answered.

Please he begged. No! I don't want anyone I replied. His cousins and his uncle had to drag him away. As they dragged him away he was saying. "We'll look after each other, we'll help each other." At that they were taken away by the police. Later I was to find out it was to work at a railway station.

Chapter Eleven

Life as Enforced Labour

Now I'm going to tell you of life at Opladen. This town is near Dusseldorf. It was the first factory we were taken to as a labour force. It was called Blechwarenfabrik and I was there officially from April 1942 to January1943. (This includes the period of imprisonment in Munich).

r Zeichen   Unser Zeichen   Opladen, den
                   B/Hs.   2o. Januar 1947

     Wir bescheinigen hiermit
Katharina Demenschenko, jetzt Frau CIESLIK,
dass sie in der Zeit vom 8. April 1942
bis 31. Januar 1943 bei uns beschäftigt war-

Blechwarenfabrik
Hermann Schmitz

Telegramme: Blechschmitz Opladen · Fernruf Opladen 1024 nach Geschäftsschluß 18 95

Opladen 1947 Mama once again used her wits. Going to the Tin factory to get proof that she had been used as forced labour

We arrived at Opladen where the camp we would be staying in was situated. About 40 of us arrived, mostly from Chistakova (Torez), some from Donetsk, one or two from Stalinov. After the long days of our transport we were exhausted, cold and hungry. Our thoughts on the food we would have on our arrival.

It was late afternoon when we arrived at the camp. We were given black coffee, no bread, nothing just black coffee, ugh, nasty tasting. In the evening, our meal consisted of turnip soup. The recipe was turnip and water that was it. It didn't matter how hungry we were, we couldn't eat it, it was inedible. The German policewoman was screaming, schmeckt gut (tastes good). Essen! Essen! Cracking us at the back of the head. We still went to bed with the soup uneaten. The soup was brought to us the next day for lunch but we still couldn't eat it. (Never did hear how the soup saga ended – Lid/Vee).

I say we arrived at a camp; it wasn't a camp like the ones we would come to know. It had been a restaurant where there had been a dance hall. Beds were placed in the dance hall, barbed wire on the outside of the door. At the front of the building there was a drinking bar that the German citizens patronised. The cellars were used as kitchens. Smaller rooms were used as police accommodation. The policemen were old and there were some policewomen.

Our 40 strong group, all females, were going to work at Blechwarenfabrik Hermann Schmitz, it was a tin factory. We all realised that it was going to be tough, but somehow, we had to accept our fate. Our group were friendly and supportive. We knew we had to comfort and help one another to survive.

I remember a couple of students from Donetsk that were always kind. One of them was a tall girl her name was Zena. Everyone of our group was lovely. Our life in the camp began.

We rose early, putting our footwear of wooden clogs on that we had been given. We walked to the factory which was some distance away. One or two were chosen to work in the kitchen. My friend Vyera being one of them.

As we walked through the streets we would make a terrible noise with our wooden clogs. The Police couldn't control all of us from making a racket, although we did get, crack, crack, crack, with their sticks. The German populous started to complain as they were being woken. We made things worse for ourselves in the long run as they took us the long way round through the woods so we had to be up even earlier.

The factory wasn't bad to work for. The men in charge were lenient, apart from one Gestapo man who was there, and a German woman, who was forever reporting us, or if the mood took her she would attack us.

Every lunchtime we were brought turnip soup and water. Not being familiar with this type of work, especially the sixteen year old girls, who had been students, our hands were covered in cuts, legs cut where metal sheets had fallen. Then the long tramp back to our quarters where we were given a meagre meal. We had no rights to complain.

After some days in these austere conditions we decided not to tolerate it anymore. We came to the decision to refuse to eat or go to work. Our "strike" didn't last very long before the police were sent for. The police arrived, some of our group were beaten, some were taken away.

My personal circumstances were made more difficult by my knowledge of the German language. I started to be cross examined. "Who was the leader?" I was asked. "Who had organised the withdrawal of labour?" My answer was "everyone." "Why aren't you eating", "because if I eat I will be killed". "By whom, who will kill you?" Again I answered "everyone." They continued questioning me. When I still refused to give them information I was taken down into the beer cellar and beaten.

I and 2 other women were taken to the police station. We were locked up in the cells. The idea was to put fear into us. Crying, shouting, screaming were heard. After spending 3 days in the cells we were taken back to our "dance hall" camp.

One evening we were sat about chatting. Someone chirped up "lasses, let's run away." After some deliberation 7 of us agreed. "Right, where are we going to run to" one of the lasses enquired. "Home, back home" 2 or 3 of the voices replied. I spoke German, another girl spoke Polish. We had gathered some turnips so we had food. Collecting our trapki (rags/clothes), now we were ready for our escape.

How stupid were we? Attempting to get to Poland from Cologne. When I think about it now, we must have had no brains in our heads. With no money, no documentation, we were going to Poland. We were going to head for the station, locate a train that was going to Poland and get on it. Now to put our plan into action.

Midnight was the time we were making our getaway. There was no one guarding us (where would we go). Just a watchman who must have been asleep. Off we went heading into the countryside. Tramping through fields, stumbling through woods. Then again fields, woods. Not really knowing where we were heading. Just hoping that we'd chosen the right direction.

I was ahead of the group; the girls said it made sense as I was the only one wearing boots. If we came across any marshlands it would be easier. OK, I've got the boots so I'll go first. Eventually we ended up wandering around another wood, lost. It was before sunrise, we were traipsing through the trees when a light shone into my eyes. A voice saying "halt". Startled "whose that" I asked. The reply was "who's that". We realised we'd been caught.

Starting to act simple/naïve I replied "oh, we're going to Poland." The soldiers were out in the woodlands on manoeuvres. They looked at us and burst out into guffaws of laughter.

"To Poland, just walk straight ahead" he said. Meanwhile one of them had phoned the police headquarters. As we started to walk I heard him "we have 7 girls here, escaping to Poland." The squad led us out of the woods onto a road. Pointing ahead, one of them told us to keep on walking straight on. We would come to a station, where we would find a train bound for Poland.

Watching us for a while waiting to see that we were heading in the right direction, they then returned into the trees. We carried on down the road. Then when we knew no one was watching, we veered to the side into a field, running as fast as our legs would carry us to goodness knows where.

Our dash across the field led us to some quarries. Peering down one of them, we noted that it was very deep. The next action was to find a way down. Slipping and slithering into the quarry we found ourselves a place where we could sit and hide, where we could not be seen. But from our position we could see the top of the quarry.

A car track ran by the quarries, we got settled to try and get some rest. Vroom, vroom, motorcycles were heard. As we glanced upwards 2 police cycles were roaring back and forth. They must have been the police that had been sent to "escort" us, realising we'd run off they were searching for us. After a while they rode away and we rested a little while.

It was daylight; we climbed out of our pit and looked around. In the distance we saw what appeared to be steel/tinworks. "Right, this is what we'll do" someone said coming up with a plan. "We'll head to the steelworks and try and get a train, that way we'll get away."

Arriving at our destination, we waited at the side of the rail tracks. A goods train was approaching slowly. Luckily there were steps on the wagons. The tall girl leapt on first. Then holding her hand out to the second girl, then the third. Now it was my turn. I tried jumping up; as I was small I found it tricky. They caught my hands but the train began to pick up speed.

Faster and faster, my knees were being grazed. They had to let me go. Maria, I and another girl, whose name I can't recall, watched as the train sped off into the distance.

We got to know at a later date that the rails the train sped off on were leading to a large manufacturing plant, where thousands of "serfs" had been transported to for their labour. The train came to a stop and they realised where they were. Police came, and took them to the police headquarters.

It was a terrible place, in a cruel environment, where the workforce was treated harshly by being shot or hanged. It was a kin to a concentration camp. There was a man who'd stolen a potato. A hole was dug and filled with cold water. He was put upside down in it and left, he died like that. This was done in front of everyone, as an example to anyone who was tempted to steal. The camp, that we had run away from, was a better place to be. It was small and only 40 of us, at least we were fed turnips or cabbage in water, and on a Sunday we were given potatoes in their skins.

I can remember one occasion when they gave us some tablets that they said were vitamins. I am not sure what they really were, perhaps they were experimenting; all 40 of us came out in a rash just like chickenpox.

The 3 of us stood and watched the train disappear with our friends on board. We walked on arriving at a road, we crossed it. At the other side we stumbled across some rough terrain skirting the town eventually reaching a hedgerow. We sat down to rest, hiding ourselves amongst the greenery. Oh, it was so pleasant. Birds were serenading us, the sun was warming us with its rays, and it was so nice to be "free". Though we didn't know where our destiny would lead us.

Laying in the greenery, we drifted off into a light snooze. I awoke, hearing some sounds at the other side of the hedge. I peered through, nudging the girls, I whispered. "Look girls, police, we must be near a police station". The rest that we had just enjoyed was in the police grounds.

Waiting until no one was around; we decided to walk through the town as if we were heading to our workplace. Encircling the grounds we headed towards the town, trying not to glance about, so as not to give anyone any suspicion who we were. As we walked on we were approached from the back and were apprehended by police in plain clothes. We started to explain, trying to bluff our way out of a tricky situation.

"Don't bother lying" one of the men said. "We have your 4 friends, we were searching for you." The 3 of us were escorted to their headquarters to await the arrival of the police from the tin factory. Our 4 companions had been returned earlier, where on their arrival, they had been badly beaten. When we got back to our "camp", a beating was our share of the punishment for attempting to escape.

We continued our tedious existence, but it was not long before we were attempting to abscond again, but we had no success in our bids for freedom and were caught. Life was tough. We started strikes in our attempts to protest. When the bombings began we had no where to hide. Although the assault was not directly overhead, we heard the resounding blasts mixed with the wail of sirens. It was enough to make us fearful, edgy.

The town of Cologne which was a few kilometres from our camp was being blitzed. We could see the sky being lit, as if there were thousands of shooting stars. It was terrible, everything burning in the distance. The only means of protection we had was to crawl under the beds, or huddle together which somehow made us feel less vulnerable.

Misha from Volhovchik, who I'd met on our transport to Germany, unbeknown to me was in a camp nearby, where there was a steel mill. Beatings were also given in Misha's camp. The job he had was to travel the rails, from station to station, servicing and repairing engines. With a pass that he had been given he had more freedom than most. The rails ran from steel/tin factories to other works.

One Sunday we were being marched out on our regular Sunday walk. Passing a wired fence of a camp I heard "Katya, Katya, Tanya." When I looked I saw one of Misha's friends, Lyona, who had recognised his girlfriend Tanya, and then me through the barbed wire. Later I got to know both Misha and Lyona had been searching for us. Using the freedom that the passes issued by the authorities gave them, which allowed them travel on the rails; they had tried to find us.

"Misha has been trying to find you Katya." Lyona told me. "He got caught in a place his pass was not valid for. I was brought back here, Misha was sent to another camp." Being allowed to write to each other Lyona wrote to Misha to let him know where I was.

One morning a policewoman/guard came up to me saying Mrs Demenschenko, your husband is here." Husband, where, I haven't got a husband, my husband is dead, killed, I thought to myself. (I had documents in different names that I'd prepared at the start of the war). Curious to see who it could be, I went to the entrance. It was Misha who was stood there, holding a parcel. He had been given a permit to enter our camp. We went into our "dance hall" where we sat chatting.

Misha had brought me gifts of sugar, marmalade, bread. He had a girlfriend where he was staying, who had brought him these luxuries and he had given them to me. This was his first visit. As we sat there he took a ring out of his pocket. It was a cheap band he had managed to buy off a German. Looking at me he said "tell them I'm your husband because

I've told them (the authorities) I am." That was how my marriage began. Later we wrote each other letters and he came to see me when he could.

Mama Katya at the camp barrack

Meanwhile in our camps we organised many strikes causing as many problems as we could. We had a secret getaway behind the toilet door. There was a wire net fence that had been cut through where we managed to get out. Early mornings were the most popular time to go pilfering. Taking turns we climbed through the slit in the wire. After getting apples, pears, carrots, anything edible, we brought our booty back to our camp. For a while it was rather pleasant.

Twelve Belorus girls were brought to our camp to add to the workforce. Our life continued, work, sleep, walks on a Sunday for our exercise. Our secret outings to forage for food made our lives a little easier. Then things began to change. Our cupboards were searched. The strange circumstance was that every time it was the cupboard of the culprit whose turn it was to get the extras. The punishment metered out for this offence by the camp police, was not being allowed out. Everything confiscated, and no food given.

We realised that there was a traitor amongst us. As after 8 or 9 months of all living together, nothing like this had happened before. We couldn't understand why. Becoming suspicious we began to observe one another. Trying to notice anything unusual. Attention was given to a woman in our group. A large woman, with a large nose and rather ugly. It started by noticing how friendly she appeared to a female guard who was in charge. Someone noted that she was being given bread. Then she appeared in a "new" dress no one had seen before.

Our breakfast every Sunday was 2 small thin slices of bread, so meagre one gulp it was gone. After this feast we would be marched off for our

Sunday exercise, escorted by guards on pushbikes. We walked all morning until lunch time. When we returned to our "home" we were not allowed to lay on the beds that we had made in the morning, so we could not sleep, only sit on the bed, or go into the kitchen. Another alternative if it was fresh air you wanted was a fenced yard. In these adverse conditions we kept our spirits up by singing, dancing, laughing to annoy our "masters".

Fortune telling was another past-time. Our fortune teller would put some water in a dish; cover her head telling us what she could see. On one occasion, after our fortune teller had said she'd seen a man with blond hair walking across the fields, one lady burst into tears saying "It must be my husband coming back from the war safe."

The German people, who patronised the bar at the front of our "dance hall" camp, were complaining that our merriment on an evening was offensive, so we were forbidden to sing and had to stay inside the building.

An incident took place at the tin factory. A young student who was a quiet, reserved girl. A girl who no one could suspect of misbehaving or causing problems, suddenly surprised us by stating that German soldiers are bloody bastards. Her name was Nadia. Two German women heard her making this remark. One fraulein was called Tilya, the other one a large woman with a big nose, was rather ugly, an unpleasant type of person. One of her games that she found amusing, was to walk up to one of the workers and slap them, then she'd burst out laughing. This fraulein was called Trudy.

When Trudy heard the insult to the German soldiers made by Nadia she went to the authorities and reported what she had heard. The Gestapo came; he was a small short man. He went to the office and Nadia was summoned. On her return she was covered in blood, all her face battered. She had to continue working. Not long after her return there was activity in the yard. Something was being erected. Wondering what it was, we were soon to find out.

The small wooden structure was a cell just enough room to stand in. We were taken from the factory to our "home". Nadia was taken straight to the cell where she couldn't sit or lay. A metal sheet was placed in front then a bar placed across. We left her, poor girl, in the yard, cold, hungry, alone, imprisoned, that was her punishment. We were all distraught, but we couldn't do anything for her, we were helpless.

What do you think? She was in that wooden cell 3 days. Tilya the other German woman lived not far from the factory with her mother. She had no father; he had been killed at the front. On an evening when it was quiet and no one was around, Tilya would go to the factory, accompanied by her mother. The factory was in a secluded spot, a quiet area. With her mother acting as a look out, Tilya would climb over the fence, head for the cell, and unbar the door so Nadia could come out and walk around to ease her stiffness. She gave her bread and water so that her hunger pangs would be less.

The authorities were amazed that after 3 days with no sleep food or water she was still conscious. On the fourth day they unbarred the metal door to let her out. On looking inside a piece of bread was found on the floor where Nadia had accidentally dropped it. Again she was questioned as to where the bread had come from. "Someone pushed it through the gap, I didn't see who, she answered them." Nadia had served her punishment. We were warned that treatment was waiting for anyone that stepped out of line.

Still we continued to cause disruption, striking etc. I was sat at a table writing a letter to Misha when from the adjoining room I heard a commotion and screeching. It was "aunt" Lyoosya an old woman from Donetsk. Well she wasn't old, maybe 45, but we were young, so to our eyes that's how she appeared. An old policeman was beating her while a policewoman was leaning on the door, propping it shut with her shoulder. I jumped up "come on girls" I said heading to the door trying to open it. I was holding onto the door handle, my comrades behind me. We all put our weight behind the door and pushed. The door flew open, sending the policewoman sprawling. I was at the front so I was the first one to fall on top of her. The others in a pile fell after me.

Grabbing me by the hair she stood up and started beating me. The old policeman joined in pulling my hair. I grabbed hold of the door clinging to it shouting and screaming. Aware that the sound of yelling may carry to the front bar they stopped. I took my chance, running to my bed and scrambling under it. Sending everyone out of the "dance room" they tried pulling me out, shouting and cursing. They found it difficult, one of them being somewhat old. Eventually they were successful I was dragged out. The 4 of us, who had fallen into the room trying to help "aunt" Lyoosa, were taken away by the police, where we spent about a week being locked in the cells. On our return to the camp, I and the 3 girls involved were told if any of you cause disturbance or problems again you will be sent to a concentration camp.

At about the same time as this incident, it was discovered for certain that it was Maria the Belarus who was our betrayer. Some of the girls bided their time, then one night she was covered in a blanket and beaten very badly. Next morning she was discovered by the policewoman barely alive. Although I and some other girls did not get involved our punishment was the same for all. No food given, not allowed into the yard, at work or at the camp. Maria the Belarus traitor was taken away immediately to another labour camp.

Chapter Twelve

Escape with Misha

The threat of being transferred to a concentration camp was now hanging over me. I wrote to Misha, as he was my "husband" he was given permission to visit me. After talking things out we decided to make plans to escape together. Our destination Poland. It was a stupid idea.

The railways he worked on also had German workers. Not all Germans were bad. Some of the German co-workers were very sympathetic. Workers working together had camaraderie of a kind. Misha had saved up some marks from the pittance he was paid. At the factory we were paid pence's so I had a small amount of cash. We put our plans into action.

Misha had managed to obtain a lady's velvet coat, fancy hat, some nice underwear, handbag and gloves from one of his German colleagues, whose wife they belonged to. Whether she knew he'd taken her coat and hat, and where, I'll never know. Misha managed to get these items to me on a visit. Our respective camps were on the opposite sides of the town Cologne. On the following night we helped him into our camp through the secret gap that we had used for our foraging into the country side.

When I told the girls they started crying, saying whose going to stick up for us now. I said you will have to look after yourselves. If I stay here I will be sent to a concentration camp. At least if I go to another camp they'll not know my history.

Hiding him in our "dance hall" bedroom that night, I also prepared for my escape, wrapping my hair in rags so that my hair was curly the next day, not bedraggled. With the freedom to travel on the railway Misha's permit gave him, we were ready, marking time till the train started to run, taking the labourers, office workers etc to their posts.

We came out of the camp through our secret exit in the fence outside the toilet door. Looking rather smart with my wavy hair, new coat and fine hat, we headed through the garden and to a street, making our way towards the railway station, as if we were part of the German populous. Arriving at the station we bought our tickets and got on the train.

The train was passing near the area where Misha was currently working – Oberhausen. Arriving at our stop we got off the train, making our way to a workman's hut at the side of the tracks. Leaving me there he made his way back to his barracks.

On his return, he was given a beating after it had been discovered he'd not been in the camp all night. I was to go to the police and tell them I'd been left behind by the train.

I changed my decent clothes into my old coat. After spending the night alone in the hut, I put on a headscarf and stepped out of the worker's hut into the early morning air. My next goal was to find a policeman to tell my sorry tale to.

Travelling through the town, clean air, birds singing it was so pleasant. The Rhine flows through some beautiful places, if you are free to enjoy it, but if like me, you're afraid to walk down the street, the beauty is dimmed.

A policeman was walking towards me, wheeling his pushbike. He looked at me and I asked him the way to his base. He pointed the way to go and went off. I continued on the road to where he'd pointed out.

Arriving at the police station I went in, it appeared to be deserted. I stayed there wondering if someone would arrive. Eventually after many hours, in walked the elderly policeman who had pointed the way I was to go.

Looking surprised he said "It was 5.00am when she asked where the station was and she's still here!" It was maybe 9.00pm. I was taken to another part of the building. I had to wait for the Commandant who was to interview me.

A small elderly man with a moustache came into the room, followed by an interpreter; she worked at the hospital I think. I was asked what had happened. I began to tell them but the interpreter started to twist my words. I quietly said to her in Russian, "Listen! you tell him what I'm telling you to tell him. If you damage me my friends will pay you back." She went as red as a beetroot. The Commandant kept saying to the interpreter, "what is she saying, what is she saying?" The interpreter started to translate my words correctly. I explained that I was on a train, and had got off for some fresh air and the train had left without me. I told a pack of lies, I can't even remember what they were, but I was successful at lying my way through.

The Commandant was so kind. I was weeping, sobbing, "I don't know where my husband is, I've had nothing to eat all day, my parents are Austrian "descendants", I wailed, "but I was taken as a Russian.". Descendants from the Austro Hungarian empire whose lineage was Austrian were still known as Austriti.

Looking concerned the Commandant told me not to get upset. It was lunchtime and he took me to his house. The house had a veranda where I was seated. In waddled his wife, a large frau maybe 20 stone. Sat there in my old clothes, puffed eyes from weeping, it was obvious to her that I was a foreigner from the forced labour force. "Why have you brought her here?" she yelled at him. He started to explain that my parents were Austrian and my circumstances and his wife calmed down.

They had a 19 year old son who was at home on sick leave as he had been wounded at the front. He came and sat with me and we started chatting, he spoke a little Russian/Ukrainian, I German. After chatting for a while I understood why his father had been kind to me. He had told his father when he was stationed in the Ukraine the local people were kind to him giving him milk and bread saying "what are you doing lad, this is no place for you, you're still young, go home." Although it was forbidden to speak like this about the enemy, a father's heart understood why his son liked the Ukrainians,

Everything I had told the Commandant he believed, so he made arrangements for my next employment. That evening I was taken to a marmalade/jam factory nearby. Giving my benefactor the information that was needed for my new documentation, which would be delivered when ready. That was when I changed my name to Misha's surname Teclik. The surname I had used was false anyway, (Demenschenko).

The director of the marmalade factory was a fine man, fair. The barracks we lived in were small, sited on the banks of the Rhine. Twelve girls occupied them, also there were 2 pilots, good looking young men, who had been captured and had escaped. Misha came that evening to the barracks. No police or guards were on duty, only an old lady who looked after things. The food we were fed was good, the work in the factory not hard, conditions agreeable. I thought I was in paradise, but paradise didn't last long for me.

The search for me had begun. I was not that easy to find, as the jam factory was a distance from Cologne, nearer to Bonn and of course I had changed my surname. Mishka was the one who had visited me, also I had written to him. He was the one with a pass, so suspicion fell on him, as having helped me escape from the tin factory. He had started to be beaten to try and find out my whereabouts. I stayed in my new place about 2 or 3 weeks, enjoying the easier life.

There was a dance hall where we arranged our leisure time such as singing and dancing. In this hall a wedding had been arranged for me and Misha. A priest blessed us and married us, it was lovely. Misha would visit when possible and our own lads were there. It was good, so much better than the last camp I'd been at. Misha had decided it was time to carry on with our escape, our destination, Poland.

On the day we decided to start our journey, I gathered my belongings and headed for the hut on the track, where I and Misha had arranged to meet. He wasn't there. I went into the hut to wait for him. As I sat there, drones of aeroplane engines were heard, sirens wailing, a bombing raid had started. Everything around appeared to light up as if it was daylight, fires started raging. In the distance a large factory was on fire. The noise of explosions and sirens, the ground appeared to move, everything shaking, lights flashing as if it was a firework display. Laying on the floor of the hut on my own I huddled up and waited. The all clear siren was heard, the raid had ended.

I sat up, pulling myself together, I tidied myself, getting changed into my finery, the coat and fancy hat, tearing my photos and documentations into small pieces so if caught they wouldn't know my identity. Hearing a train stopping in the distance, I waited. The workers had arrived. Misha hurried ahead of them. "Oh you're here" he gasped sounding relieved.

Making our way back to the station we bought tickets to make our way home via Poland. It was just prior to Christmas the weather drizzly and cold. Our first destination was Hanover. Getting on the train we set off on our journey

Reaching Hanover we got off our train to organise our next route. On the station we got chatting to some West Ukrainians. Because in the past they had been ruled by Austria, West Ukrainians had freedom of travel, as had Austrians, they could travel home on holidays, back to West Ukraine. Unknown to me at this time, West Ukraine had divisions that were with the Nazis. If from East Ukraine then your classification was Russian. I was classed as Russian (Ukrainian). Many males from East Ukraine were given an option of saying they were Ukrainian, if they took the option they would then join Ukrainian sections attached to German battalions. A few took the opportunity others refused.

Anyway, they advised us not to go the way we had planned as security was high, Dachau being in that vicinity. "OK" Misha said "We'll head for Switzerland." Mishka had some money, he and his accomplices who worked the railway, stole from train carriages, wheeling and dealing. He'd got money for the tickets which weren't expensive. Our destination Muchen/Munich.

We travelled all night. Everything was alright until we arrived near Neurenberg. Misha had dozed off, sitting by his side I noticed Gestapo approaching. They were in civilian clothes and were checking passengers' documents.

Misha had our papers. "Misha, Misha" I whispered digging him with my elbow trying to wake him. "Err, err", he muttered. They came up to us "Pass! pass!" they said. Misha, half asleep reached into his pocket pulling out the documents, he gave them to the Gestapo. Instead of giving them his travel pass, he had given them the documents where he worked, where we were running away from.

Chapter Thirteen

Captured by the Gestapo – Munich Prison

The train stopped at Nuremberg, we were not taken off there, later continuing the journey to Munich. We got off the train our journeys end. We were not handcuffed, and were told to walk ahead, escorted by the 2 Gestapo. We were instructed not to look back or run or we would be shot. Maybe they suspected we were going to be met by conspirators. Two more Gestapo came up to us, we were now surrounded by 4 captors.

It felt like a long time had passed as we stood on that station at Munich. A Black Maria came to a stop near us. My heart sank, "that's it Misha" I exclaimed, "this is our Switzerland and Poland!" My stomach was in knots, the realisation had hit me that we were in the Gestapo's hands. Now a life of prison begins.

Opening the doors of the black van we were pushed into the back, I was holding on to Misha, there were some prisoners inside. Maybe because we were well dressed, voices started calling out from all sides, asking if we had any bread or food for them to eat. The van set off, arriving into a yard, large gates opened up before us. Our ordeal had started (oy, yoy yoy! what we lived through).

At the entrance we were parted, males went one way, females the opposite direction. I didn't see Misha again until the next day when we were being questioned.

The cell I was locked in was spacious. My cellmates were different nationalities, Polish, French, Belgium, Belarus, Russian and Ukrainian. If you were from East Ukraine you didn't differentiate between Russian and Ukrainian to us it was classed as all the same.

The girls came up to me straight away, lovely girls they were, friendly. All the girls were inside prison for varying reasons. One very pretty woman, a brunette had been arrested because she had fallen in love, her name was Maria.

Maria had worked as a servant in a gentleman's household. A soldier who had been in the Ukraine, had just returned and was staying at the house, as he was a relative of the gentleman. His experiences in the Ukraine had been good and he was full of praise for the Ukrainian people. Meeting Maria, he liked her on first sight, he took her to the cinema and they began to secretly meet. Fate was against them.

They got caught out. Both of them were arrested. His cell was on the opposite side to us, situated on a corner but if we hoisted her up on our shoulders she could shout to her German sweetheart through the barred cell windows. There were a few occasions when we would hear the guard's footsteps hurrying to our cell. Then she would receive a smack or thump at the back of her neck for communicating with him.

Another girl had run away from a farm she worked at. The reason being, to search for her brother. She was taken for interrogation. When she was returned back to the cell, she had a broken nose, her poor eyes were swollen, red and beginning to bruise. We thought she had committed a heinous crime to be so badly beaten. Her misdemeanour was that she refused to reveal which farm she had absconded from. The beating she received was so severe, she was taken away. She was not seen again, so I don't know what happened to her.

A tall beautiful West Ukrainian girl, slim, with lovely long plaits, was a girl that would sit apart from everyone, huddled in a corner, head down, eyes lowered. I think she was called Halya, she was beautiful. It was heartbreaking to watch her crouching all the time repeating the same phase, "what will my mama say?" what will my mama say?" I think she had lost her mind a little; she refused to eat or drink. When the soup was brought to us we would take her dish to have it filled, then between us trying to hold her down, to try and get a little food and water inside her.

Lots of problems were caused by the Polish and French girls trying to take her soup and bread away from her. I think maybe she was with child and was afraid of being sent away. (Maybe back to West Ukraine?). After about a week the police came and took her away. I hope she found someone who was kind to her as we'd been.

Rising early in the morning we had to fold our mattresses which had been placed on the floor. About 50 people resided in the cell. There was water and a toilet inside the cell. The adjoining prison room was smaller; it was used as a short term stay place, where new prisoners were brought in for questioning, then taken away, so there was a steady change of faces.

I was in that prison, hanging about, maybe 6 months. It was a traumatic time. I saw things I find difficult to repeat. What helped me survive was my knowledge of the German language, also knowing how to use my wits.

At this point, girls in our cell hadn't been sentenced. We had been taken in for interrogation. On a morning some of us would be chosen to do prison chores. I always tried to be one of the first in line at the barrier when our cell door was opened. One group would be taken down to the cellars to sort out potatoes, beetroot, now and again carrots would be amongst the vegetables we were sorting. Another group were taken to work in the kitchens and clean the canteen.

I've forgotten a lot of individual cases. One girl had been arrested when it had been discovered that she had been writing a diary, recording her days. Russian, Ukrainian, Belarus, the Soviet group would sit in one corner, to pass away the hours. I would read the cards and tell fortunes, or we would play card games, also telling each other anecdotes to keep our spirits up. Somehow it helped me forget my predicament for a while, when I was trying to cheer up someone else. The smokers in our group were always happy at my small harvest of cigarette ends, that I had gathered whilst sweeping the canteen floor.

In the other corner Polish girls were together, then the French group. A Belgian girl was in our cell; maybe a Jewish girl, because some of the French and Polish girls would abuse her by sneering and taunting, "you're a Jewess". "No" she would deny, saying "I am a Belgian." It was a pity to see them acting this way to another human being who was in the same situation as themselves. The "Soviet" group tried to defend her but were almost beaten by them.

The bread that we were given in the evening we would hide under our pillows so that the following morning we would have something to eat. On waking we would discover the precious bread had disappeared. Either the Poles or the French had somehow managed to pilfer it. The result of the bread theft was that we had to go hungry all day, waiting for the hour the soup was dished out in the evening.

About the soup. As I'm retelling this I'm remembering that soup and thoughts creep unwilled into my mind. When the soup was brought to us the aroma that drifted from it was lovely. As we ate it the taste was delicious or so it seemed to us, plenty of meat. The meat was some type of intestine, but we ate it, we were hungry, no matter how it looked or what it was. Now! I think. Wartime meat was short so what was that soup made of? Rabbit? Dog? Cat?, maybe even human. Pigs and cows don't have guts such as they were in that soup. The meat pieces were of the size of small fingers, so I suppose I will never know what that soup that kept us alive was made of.

Some of the French or Polish, oh! I don't know what nationality they were, but they would kiss and caress each other. Then do terrible things (sex?). Now I know what was happening with some of the girls. Though at the time it has to be remembered, 40 years ago, the average youth was very naïve. We would keep out of the way hiding in our corner, afraid, not understanding why they were behaving in such a lewd, vulgar manner. We decided they must be depraved women who were prostitutes. In prison life is seen in the raw, evil and good.

Our "Soviet" group consisted of 10 souls. There were more in number of the Polish Austrian women. Though I'm not sure what their nationality was, they used to call themselves "Handlyoky". We had no contact with them, but could hear their conversations. I was in that cell a long time …….. witnessing so much horror, torture, ghosts all around this room.

A police guard would march up to the cell door holding a sheet with a list of names written down. A name was called out, that person was then taken for questioning. A couple of hours later, the cell doors were flung open and the current interrogatee would be flung in. The poor wretch, whoever it may be, had been beaten, face swollen, ribs broken, nose broken, bleeding eyes, popping out of their heads, hair dripping, wet from the dousing into water they had endured.

We would then start to clean the victim, trying to ease their pain. Every group took care of their own person. In spite of our differences, we were mostly friendly with one another as fate had dealt us all the same blow.

When I and Misha had set off on our escape it was about October 1942. By the time we had passed through different cells, our "enquiry" had begun, the date April 1943. I've told you a little about prison life, now our interrogation.

My name was called by the woman guard and I was led away to a small room where I was joined by Misha. Being told to wait, we just stood there. A door opened and a policeman called out both our names. As we entered we were faced by a woman sat behind a desk/table. She appeared middle aged, very smart and attractive. As she started to speak, I was surprised, she spoke Russian very clearly and cultured. I don't know whether she was a German or a Russian German.

She started asking us in her excellent Russian about our documentation. I of course had destroyed mine. Answering her questions truthfully, the only lie we told was that we were husband and wife and because we weren't together, we had run away. Her questions were asked in a very civilised manner. She was very pleasant to us as she listened to our explanations.

Opposite, facing where we were sat there was a large door, which was open onto a room which then led to a third room. The scene that we were looking at was unnerving. Behind a desk, a Gestapo man was seated, opposite him stood a young man, flanked by 2 guards (policemen). I say young man; he looked as if he was a boy 16, maybe 17 with a wiry build. All we could see was his back, slightly stooped, head bent.

As he stood there one policeman would hit him at the side of his head, then the other would repeat the action from his side, knocking him off his feet. Raising him on his feet, they would continue the process; all the while the boy was having questions barked at him from the Gestapo man sitting behind the desk. What questions were being asked couldn't be heard, we were not near enough, but we heard the boy's yelps of pain.

The woman scrutinised us, saying, "tell me the truth, if you tell me the truth, then I will help you, but! if you lie and your lie is discovered, then your next visit is there." Her finger was pointing at the room where we were witnessing the lad being questioned by the Gestapo. "Then it will be too late for me to do anything" she informed us.

Now! After that interview we were both taken back to our respective cells. I didn't seen Misha again until the following day, when again we were taken for interrogation. The same questions were repeated, then we were returned to our prison room.

Later I discovered Misha had been sent to a concentration camp. When they took Misha away I was frightened. I tried to hang myself with a scarf, but failed. A police woman had entered the room and saved me. I had grazed my neck. "Why are you doing this?" she asked, "because I'm afraid of the concentration camp" I whimpered." "If you tell the truth you won't be sent there" she snapped. That's how it was – sigh.

Misha had been transported to a concentration camp near Munchen/Munich. In the future he was to tell me about the horrific conditions in that camp. They were put to labour when not engaged in various tasks. They were ordered to sit at a table, hands placed on the table top with instructions not to move. Dogs, Alsatians were nearby, and any small movement that was made, was a signal for the dogs to attack them. Also the beatings they received. The regime in concentration camps was very severe.

Days passed, one day being the same as another. Working in the kitchens, cleaning the cell, folding mattresses stacking them etc. High up in the cell was a slanted window. If, like acrobats, we climbed up on one another's shoulders, we could just see into the prison yard.

One time we heard groaning from outside, our window was slightly open. With the moaning, metal clanging could be heard. Doing our acrobat gymnastics we climbed on each others shoulders. I being the smallest was at the top. Grabbing the edge of the window frame I looked into the yard. Oh! My goodness! People, just skin and bone were shuffling along, chains on their ankles, their hands were not bound, but they were having difficulty getting into the trucks on the steps that led them up to the back of the truck. All the while being pushed with the batons the guards had in their hands.

A police guard glanced up, then walked away. "Ah" I thought, he didn't see me. Then footsteps were heard running down the corridor. He had phoned the cell gates reporting what he had seen. Jumping down, I fell on the floor, just as the keys were jangling in the cell door lock. Somehow she passed me by, another girl got the punches.

That's how life passed in the cell. Day by day not knowing what was awaiting you, what the future held. The time I spent in that prison was very difficult. Tortured victims thrown into the cell, new prisoners arriving, some prisoners departing.

Late Autumn 1943, yet another bombing raid. Part of the prison was on fire and we were herded down into a large cellar. I don't know why they took us down to the cellar, they didn't care whether we would live or die. In the cellar were gypsies, men, women and children. As we entered there hell had broken lose. The men who'd been on one side and the women and children who had been kept on the other side ran to each other. The police were beating them, trying to separate them. Men, woman and kids were crying and screaming (mama in tears remembering). I'll never forget it. They were cuddling each other; they knew they were going nowhere – only to the crematorium. I don't know how long they'd been imprisoned, or what time they had left. Once the bombing stopped we were taken back to our cells.

I'm telling you from my personal experience, I would always opt for a male police guard than a female guard. Whether it was in camps, prison or workplace, to me the female was always more severe when they had power.

One day a policewomen came to the cell. "Frau Teclik! Get ready for transport" she snapped. Where and why I didn't know. Then a little later she told me she thought my husband was being brought back, and we were to be returned to where we had absconded. The lady who had questioned us remembered and helped us, keeping her word. This was to be the first time I would see Misha since our meeting at the interrogation.

Two of us were leaving on this transport at this time. We were in tears when the time came to part from the girls left behind in the prison. Three more girls were to join us; one of the girls was one of the girls we were parted from at Frankfurt.

Leaving the cell, and entering the corridor holding my few possessions in a bundle, I looked ahead. Two lines of people met my gaze; in one line were females in the other males. They were being categorised to which destination they were heading, being prepared for transportation. I walked up to them, "my husband should be here," I said, searching with my eyes down the file of men. I had saved some black bread we had been given that morning; also I had managed to get cigarettes and matches along with the tobacco I had collected from the cigarette ends I had swept up.

As I walked down the line passing the men, I heard, "Katya" from one of the men I had just gone past. I turned around and went back, the policeman didn't stop me. The voice I recognised. "Misha?" I looked at him. This man was hardly recognisable. His hair had grown long, lank, unkempt, he was unshaven, his thin body was just skin and bones. Tears running down my cheeks, I passed him the bread and tobacco. A moment later the police guard told me to stand on the opposite side in the women's line.

We were loaded on to the trucks. When our journey in the trucks ended, we were unloaded, then we had our wrists handcuffed in pairs. Woman tied to woman, man to man. Another trek had started.

Chapter Fourteen

RETURN TO COLOGNE

Marching us to the train wagons where our hands were set free, we were loaded onto the train. This train had appeared to be specially designed for transporting prisoners. A corridor with cubicles leading off. In the cubicles there was a small window at the side.

We were put into these compartments which held 4 persons. Unable to sit or lie so we would take it in turns to kneel so that our legs could have a rest, as we were packed like sardines in a tin. Police guards strolled up and down the corridor.

Our journey from Munich took us through lovely countryside which we could see through the small window, green forests, hills. Eventually after travelling all day, our train stopped, it was just before evening. We were loaded off the train. Our wrists handcuffed so that we were in pairs and we were marched off.

Being weak from our confinement the march was taxing. Women appeared a little stronger than the men. (Maybe the men were weakened by the conditions of the concentration camps?) Some of the men stumbled or fell, but had to raise themselves and keep walking. I remember the walk from that train as if it were yesterday. Stumbling along for maybe an hour and a half, but it felt like a long time, we hadn't any strength.

I was supporting an elderly lady who was finding it difficult to walk. As I was handcuffed to her I had to keep helping her to keep up the pace with the group. Making our way through a built up area, then passing fields and hills. Eventually we arrived at some tunnels that led into the hills.

Entering the tunnel we kept on walking. The tunnel was long, dark, a light shone in the distance. How long we walked through those tunnels I don't know, but it was as if we would never arrive or reach that glow.

Finally we arrived to where the light was coming from. Entering a passage way, it was a long corridor. There were numerous soldiers, military of varying ages stood about. We were led to what appeared a type of large cage with sliding doors. All the females were marshalled in. Where the males were taken I don't know. The place we had been brought to was obviously a type of military base.

Our transportation was carried out in such a way. Travel a day then wait one day, two days a week? until the next transport was available. We were locked in the cage so we couldn't escape. On leaving our last prison we had been given a loaf of bread and a small piece of wurst (type of sausage), this was to last 3 days.

One of the soldier guards appeared to be pleasant, a late middle aged man, so I plucked up courage to ask him about my husband. "Name?" he asked, "Teslik", I answered. He walked away returning with Misha through a sliding hatch. I passed half the load that I had to him we stood and talked a few minutes. The guard started joking with us. "Kiss one another!" he laughed. "Go on, why don't you kiss each other?". You're jeering at us, we don't know where we are heading, or what is going to happen to us, I thought, feeling anger.

There were other groups of inmates in this large enclosure. Now I realise they were the females who preferred their own sex. They would kiss, embrace, I can't tell you what I saw, but to my eyes it was vulgar. Their behaviour should have been private, discreet. Another group appeared to be ladies of easy virtue.

Soldiers stationed there were many. These "ladies" would approach the guards on duty and through the wire net would offer their services with lewd suggestions and actions, lifting their dresses saying cheeky things. (I shouldn't have said this, as it wasn't that important). Returned later with cigarettes giggling. (Try and understand I grew up mostly in rural life, where behaviour such as this was unheard of, never mind witnessed. Village people tended to be moral and respectful).

Fed with soup and bread, we were caged for 2 days, and then we were let out of cell and prepared for our continuing transportation. Wrists were handcuffed to another person so we walked in pairs, then we were marched back through the tunnels we had entered 2 days previous.

Reaching our departure point I still had not seen Misha. I then noticed the men being loaded on to the train. We, the women followed them on to the wagons. Though it was for prisoners to be moved, the layout differed from the other train we had arrived in. These were wagons that we were packed into, not carriages with cell compartments. I cannot remember whether there was space to sit, but we travelled through the night and the following day finally the wagons came to a halt.

Nuremberg was the place we had stopped at. We were ordered off the train and taken to our place of confinement. Leading us to a large room below, where straw had been placed on the ground. The selection process began, to place us in different cells.

As they examined us it was discovered my head, clothes, everything was full of lice as was Maria's. I was led upstairs, Maria was taken elsewhere. On my arrival at the top I was taken to a place and disinfectant power was sprayed all over my head, my body, my clothes. After this procedure I was put in a small cell. In this cell there was no bed only a bucket, a broken window let in the cold air.

Staring at the walls I saw it was covered with previous occupant's names and various messages. I started to cry I was frightened. My sobbing turned into sounds of a dog howling, I couldn't calm myself. A song was being song somewhere. Listening there was a tapping, a beat accompanied the singing. A man's voice called "Dyevooshka! Dyevooshka!" (young woman) in Russian.

"Who are you young woman?" "Why are you crying?" Who are you young woman?" "What's your name?" "Go closer to the window, then we can hear one another, we can talk." I approached the broken window. The voices were coming from a cell that was next door.

"Don't cry" I heard. "We'll see you tomorrow." I explained how we had escaped our labour camp and were being returned. A man's voice replied "don't cry, you have a chance of life, we don't know what is waiting for us, maybe death." I listened as he continued. "Don't be afraid, you can talk, up here there's only Fritz on duty, he's a good sort, downstairs it's different." Hearing humour in the voice as he added, "they're all probably hiding in the bunkers."

Morning dawned; doors were being opened so that the inmates of the cells could get a wash and empty buckets that had been used as toilets. The policeman opened my cell. As I stepped through the doorway the men from my neighbouring cell surrounded me. They were Soviet prisoners of war, maybe 16 of them. Apparently they had been sent to labour at an airbase in Nuremberg. By their leather jackets it could be recognised they were pilots.

I can't remember the details of what they told me. They had been making plans to escape and sabotage. Somehow someone had got the information and had denounced them, sold them down the river. "Three of us have already been shot. We are awaiting our sentence, prison or death" one of them told me.

How terrible to witness such scenes.

They were fine men. On a morning when we had ablutions, we would chat, I had comrades with me, though maybe death was waiting for them. Still on an evening, singing voices could be heard coming from their cell. Brave men who kept their spirits up with song.

After the war, if I had put a search out for them by adverts in the newspaper, maybe I would have discovered their fate. But we were too afraid to contact home or be heard of, so searching for someone was not a good idea.

The morning arrived when I had to part from my friends, who had supported me, comforted me when I was frightened, distraught in the dark nights.

Frankfurt/Koblentz

After the same procedure, wrists chained in pairs, shouting at us, prodding and pushing us to move faster. If you were fastened to an older person, it was even more difficult trying to speed up, when your companion was slow, finding it difficult to walk.

Leaving Nuremberg I realised we were getting nearer to the place we had run away from, not the concentration camp I had dreaded so much. Here I get a little confused whether it was Frankfurt or Koblentz we arrived at.

Two of us were led to a great hall, Maria being the other one. Our companion transportees had been led off in another direction. The hall was enormous, with room for 200, maybe more people. Two rows of bunk beds were placed close together. It was evening as we were being led to the bottom of the room. The lights were so dim we could only just see where we were walking.

Reaching the very end of this hall, we were given blankets and shown our beds which were placed in a corner. Before marching away, the policeman said, "If lights go on or you hear whistles, bells, don't get out of bed, just cover your heads, get under the blanket, it will not concern you," then marched off. In this hall with high ceilings again I was destined to witness harsh treatment of one human being to another.

The bunks that were lined in the hall were wooden, no mattress or blanket. A toilet of some type, and a round basin, which contained water. These wooden bunks were occupied by Jewish women, young and old. The youngest being maybe seventeen, no children were there.

As they were climbing into their bunks to sleep a policeman would enter, blowing a whistle. At this they had to jump out of the bunks and stand in pairs at the front of their "beds".

Walking down the centre of the hall he would count them. As he was leaving the whistle would be blown again. They had to climb back on to their wooden shelves. Younger women were at the top, the less able at the bottom. If anyone was struggling there was always help from one of their companions who were near.

An hour, maybe two would pass. Lights switched on, whistle blown again, the count again, the whistle and scramble to get some rest. This inhumane treatment continued throughout the night. How can one human being do that to another human being and find enjoyment in it.

Water was brought to them in the morning. Being very thirsty they nearly choked, gulping it. Dinner time, again some type of liquid was brought to them. I never saw any bread being given, everything that was given to consume was a kind of liquid

Maria and I were there 2 days. The only thoughts that kept running through my head were, "God help me! Why? Why?" we would say to one another. "Can it be true, they are suffering because Christ had been crucified", answering ourselves, "But that was 2000 years ago! These people are innocent, blameless, poor people, poor wretches. Though we were prisoners we had the chance to survive."

These poor souls were on route to concentration camps. I have often wondered if any of them survived. We were in that place 2 days. I thought I would go out of my mind, but now this journey had ended, the next began.

Misha and I had not met since the meeting when I passed him bread. Nuremberg was the last time I'd had a glimpse of him, when we were being led to the wagons, but it was at a distance, we couldn't communicate. Main stations where we stopped transportees were taken to different groups depending on where their final destination was, so there were less of us than had started out.

Another prison to wait for the next stage of our "trek", to Cologne. A policeman led me down a few steps to a cellar, only a few short steps, here he left me. There was a light on as I looked I saw a metal structure. Always having an inquisitive nature (nosey), I walked towards it to take a look. I suppose the policeman didn't think I'd be that curious.

Inside was a stone bed and a stone pillow. This steel "hut" was covered in holes. What to me appeared like bullet holes covering the walls. Realising it was some type of chamber for punishment; I started shaking, petrified with fear. Feeling as if spirits were flying around, watching me pressing down on me.

Hearing footsteps, after an hour or half an hour of this ghostly experience, I felt happy relief as the policeman gave me orders to follow him. Loading us on our transport off we went.

That was the last of those terrifying cells and prisons. Witnessing the horrific suffering of humanity that I had seen in those prisons. You think that's the end. No! I will be telling of more torments to be endured. Now I continue.

Out of Prison

We arrived in Cologne, it had been badly bombed. Most bombing raids were carried out at night, lightening the heavens with fire and explosion. A policeman entered the room where I was joined by Misha, we were stood waiting for what fate had in store. "You are free from prison Herr & Frau Teclik" he stated, "You are now going back to work!"

I shuddered dreading my return to the tin factory. In walked a man holding papers (documents) in his hand. He was the one that was going to escort us back to work. As we walked out of the police station to breathe fresh air, hands or legs not bound it felt well.

Chapter Fifteen

FARM LABOUR

Now we were told we were going to meet our new master. The train we were travelling on took us past beautiful views. Hills dotted with houses. They may have belonged to wealthy people, poor folk or farmers. Still to my eyes so picturesque. Valleys with winding rivers flashed past, finally arriving at Essen.

So now we arrive at our new master's home. I spoke German, my husband was a competent man who had knowledge and the ability to be a driver, mechanic and electrician, so a handy fellow to have around.

Misha our Dad also could play Spanish guitar and sing. Katya our mam was a wonderful singer, remembering songs from years gone by when she was a girl back in her homeland. (Lidiya).

The place we had been brought to was a small farm. Arriving at the house there was an old man and woman stood there to meet us. By their side was their son and daughter in law, they didn't have any small children. It was a nice place. A river ran down one side, tree covered hills on the other. Fresh air filling our lungs. My foot always caused me pain, discomfort, as my heel had never had a chance to heal. I was on my feet more that resting them. Our work began.

Our room was above the wash house. We were given a pirina (feather quilt). Mishka didn't have it so bad his duties was to repair motors on tractors etc, repair fences, deliver milk to the station for collection. The mistress taught me how to milk cows, my hands would get red and sore from this chore. My mistress had also pointed out a cow in the herd that gave out the richest milk. When I was milking this cow I would indulge myself drinking the creamy liquid. Noticing the cow's yield had dropped they must have had their suspicions as I was never allowed to milk that cow again.

It was pleasant on the farm. Dawn starts to break, the sun just waking. After milking the cows, cleaning the cow shed was next on the list, which wasn't an easy task, clearing dirty straw, covered in cow dung. Pigs were also reared on the farm. When the days were rainy I had to chop wood, but the German family all worked hard. The son the daughter-in-law, although the old lady just saw to the house and cooking meals. The old man, liked most old men, just pottered about. Dinner breaks I would go up to my room with Misha, passing the time by de-lousing each other, looking into each other's hair.

One day I was scratching myself, pulling at my hair, my mistress was nearby. I pulled out a louse saying to her "look, I have lice, showing her what I had between my fingers." "Brrrr," she shuddered all over and left. A short time had past she returned from the house. In her arms she was carrying a small pile of clothes; they were for me and Misha to change into. The wash house held a large boiler, we were given the day off to clean ourselves. All our belongings were placed in the boiler. I wore a dress that my mama had made me, also a blouse that she had embroidered at the time she was wounded. I rarely took them off, as I was afraid these precious items would be stolen.

Left – Mama Katya in the blouse her mother embroidered.

The dress is still in daughter Lidiya's possession and now in a Barnsley museum. The blouse in daughter Vyera's possession.

Into the boiler went our lice covered belongings. My dress the colours faded, and the colours ran on the embroidery of my blouse. What upset me is that whilst most of the clothes I'd been wearing ever since I'd left home survived, the big white shawl disintegrated. At first I thought someone had stolen it. I called to my mistress and said "someone has stolen my shawl". Never! She replied. She got a big stick and stirred the clothes round in the boiler. All that was left of my shawl was pieces of ragged material. She was a kind woman, and life on this farm wasn't bad.

Now I'll continue and tell you of my experiences. Some were pleasant and happy others difficult. The farm was set in a pretty setting. Nearby was a small village, a river flowed past and hills in the background, as if protecting this small idyll from the horror we had left behind. I had to rise as dawn was breaking to milk the cows. It was no hardship to breathe the country air and drink my fill of fresh milk. The owners were not severe and we were given a good dinner every day. The difficulty was that we were not free and didn't know how long we would live this comfortable way of life.

My leg started to swell as my injury hadn't healed. As I cleaned the cow shed or chopped wood I cried with the pain I was in. I found it difficult to carry on with the work so a doctor was sent for. After looking at my leg pronounced "she can't do heavy labour." The master of course needed workers; he had no other relatives to help. Cowsheds had to be cleaned, the cows had to be milked, wood to chop, gardens to dig, in spring, fences to repair, in autumn potatoes to sort in the cellar. The tasks were endless.

A memory has just drifted back as I mention the cellar.

Prior to my leg swelling I had worked out a scheme of how to supplement our food. A wide pipe led from the wash house below our room to the cellar. For some reason the pipe was lagged and the end of the pipe covered in material. I was crafty. Whenever I was send to the cellar to sort potatoes or other chores, I took advantage. It may have been war time but the cellar was full of stores. Tins of meat, apples, pears. I would help myself to small amounts of the stock. A couple of apples or a tin of meat. Removing the material from the end of the pipe, I would stash my gains inside; replace the rags that covered the end, always making sure I left no empty spaces on the shelf, so my theft wasn't discovered. As I went back to our room after a day's toil I would reach into the pipe in the wash house and retrieve the prize.

After we had finished our daily chores, we could stroll to the nearby village, where other male and female workers would go, get to know each other, and make new friends. Though not "free" we felt no restrictions, no one keeping an eye on us, no one guarding us. Life was good, but not for long. Such happiness doesn't last.

After the doctor said I was unfit for heavy work, the owner didn't want me, but wanted Mishka, my husband, as he was useful to him. Misha could fix electrics, drive, repair tractors and cars, but now I was useless to him, I was being sent away. My husband started to kick up a fuss; he said he wanted to be with his wife. To save problems the farmer relented also letting Mishka go.

We were sent to the labour office. In our hearts there was a fear, a niggle, as to where we would next be sent. Another farm, or a camp, or maybe a factory? No, our next place of work was a restaurant.

Chapter Sixteen

Working in Restaurant

I was put in the kitchen to wash pots, clean the floors, a general dogsbody. A head woman, her daughter and daughter in law ran the restaurant as their husbands were in the army. The head woman had a son who had a farm, that was the place Misha had to work. My husband's health was not too good. He was also sensitive to unpleasant smells. One of his jobs was to clean out manure and slurry, and at this he would be sick and came to me telling me how wretched he was, and he couldn't cope, but he had no choice.

My situation working in the kitchen was not bad. The restaurant was a nice place, it stood on a corner. French Vichy officers would go there to dine. The young women, with their husbands away serving in the army, would flirt and carry on with the officers. Enjoying the attention that they were given. The mother would close her eyes to her daughter's antics, but noticed everything that the daughter-in-law did. Always finding fault with all she did. This of course caused friction between them, they were forever arguing.

For me it was comfortable, if only I kept my nose out of other people's business, did my work quietly and did not draw attention to myself. But when I saw injustice I always had to open my mouth. I was fed decent food, had a bed in the attic which was warm, so I was getting by OK. My tendency to help people brought me difficulties. I stole to give to others less fortunate than I.

I was beaten for strikes at the factory where I first worked – why? Because I refused to inform. As the one who spoke German I was chosen for questioning. My answer was always, "I don't know." As all 40 of us couldn't be arrested the work in the factory would suffer. Two or three were chosen to be beaten; I was usually one of them. I hated the Nazis, not only had I lost my family, my foot damaged, but my state of mind was such that life didn't hold much meaning, so to defend the girls somehow gave me an aim. For this I was forever punished. Many times I was dragged out, beaten, my hair pulled, but I never betrayed anyone. My girlfriends who returned home (Donbas) let it be known how I stood by them.

Here mama broke away from the story; she spoke emotionally about the war and its effects.

Early mornings as I looked out of the attic window, I would see Russian/Soviet POWs being marched to their labour. The poor men looked so weary, Soviet POWs were harshly treated, Stalin refused to acknowledge them. Red Cross didn't help them. POWs of other nationalities did not get the same treatment. Russian POWs had no defenders; they were outcasts, being classed as traitors to their country, for falling into the hands of the enemy. British received Red Cross parcels, French and Belgians received parcels, but Soviets died from hunger, their country failing them. Let them not think we were the enemy for being in another land. The government of Stalin was the enemy. Let the old men that were in power then, the government, the NKVD (secret police) now look back. Twenty six million people died, not only the soldiers that fought at the front, but also the ones in POW camps. They died like flies from over work; they worked till they dropped, under fed, beaten, hungry and cold. The war ended, most were afraid to return to the "Motherland". Those that returned home were sent to penal servitude. Their crime? Being captured by the enemy. And there they stayed until it was deemed they had served their time. Whose fault was that? Not ours. I was always faithful to my country which I love. My brothers and sister whom I miss. I love England and the English people. Sent here by fate, the English people accepted me, gave us a home when our own didn't want us, denied us as traitors. Britain and other countries gave us a place to rest our heads, helped us. We were not beaten, we were not followed or spied on for having been in Germany, or that we were foreigners. Work honestly, get paid honestly. I had 6 children. My husband's health/ mind failed and he was in hospital for years. The British system helped me feed, dress and educate the children. Even though we had nothing we were not hungry. 1933 was the year when millions died in Soviet Russia, especially in the wheat belt Ukraine. They died from enforced famine. I well remember that time. How it was, what we ate. Village upon village dying of hunger. It is not propaganda, it is the truth. Let them shoot me but it's true.

End of emotional outburst. Back to story.

My attic window looked out on the street at the back of the restaurant. I gazed through the attic window, watching the Soviet POWs being marched to work by guards. Shouted at, prodded with sticks to march faster. I started to note how and when the POWs were marched past. At night when everyone was asleep, I would quietly creep down to the cellar and take what I could; mostly it was fruit and carrots. Mostly I stole carrots because there were lots of them they were not easily missed, plus they were easy to hide. To this day when I peel carrots I remember those times. Early in the morning I would sneak to the back of the house. The fence was behind a corner of the building so could not be seen easily by anyone in the house, so I was able to pass apples, pears, carrots etc through to them as they went by.

It was noticed that the stores in the kitchen cellar were being depleted. The head of the restaurant started to keep her eyes on the kitchen staff, suspecting one of them, never imagining it was I creeping about at night looting the stores. Early morning I would silently approach the fence, hearing the sound of feet tramping, approaching voices carried in the wind. Then a large number of poor POW columns being escorted by soldiers, marched to wherever they were being put to work. There were a couple of occasions when I nearly came a cropper as I passed my booty to the wretched passing war captives. One morning I stood at the railing with my bag of goodies. Some of the POWs had noticed that on some morning I was waiting for them and would walk near to the fence where I quickly passed them the food. I had just started handing out my carrots and apples and was seen by one of the policemen/guards.

At speed I started returning to the front of the building, making my way back to my attic. Too late the owner had already been woken by the policeman's loud knocking on the door. She was not happy at been woken so early in the morning. She met me at the doorway as I was returning. Angrily she started accusing me of stealing her carrots, apples pears. I denied it saying "I went out to the fence to watch them pass in the hope of seeing a familiar face. Someone from my home town." I was lucky she let me pass her, whether believing me or not, I don't know. But of course she knew that some of her stock was stolen, but didn't know who.

A little later she sent for me. She knew I'd served time in prison so was reluctant to have me arrested. She looked at me, not shouting, she spoke calmly. "You will have to go to the Harbizon" (labour office?). "I don't want to be the cause of a young woman going to prison, but I don't want you here, I don't trust you. I don't believe you, so you'll have to go."

Arriving at the labour office I met my husband. The owner's son had also got rid of him. As we were husband and wife he didn't want Misha. We sat in a little room wondering where next we would be sent.

Chapter Seventeen

Mulheim – Braun

We arrived in Mulheim I think it was. I find it difficult to remember some places. I do remember whom we were sent to serve; he was a millionaire by the name Brauer/Braun?

The house was large, set in its own grounds. At the top end of the garden was a summer house where ivy climbed up the wall. Where the pathways were there were archways entwined with apple and pear trees, it appeared as if it was a tunnel. When you entered it, the tree covered archway led to an orchard. Beyond the orchid was a large field where raspberries grew. Many a time I would sneak in, feasting on the raspberries.

The millionaire was an elderly, large man. His wife was a very small, woman and dumpy. They had one son who was serving in the army. He was stationed in the Ukraine. A number of German forces were there as it was mainly Ukraine that was occupied. The house was a mansion. The dining room had been built on a lavish scale, with large windows overlooking their grounds. Tables and chairs were set around, also easy chairs, small occasional tables by their side. A luxurious room where important guests were entertained. Here they played cards, drank, feasted, though there was a war on, it did not interfere with their pleasure.

The sitting room was also large. Braun loved to hunt, so his trophies the heads of animals, bears, deer etc were displayed on the wall in this room. It was one of these rooms that I was sent to clean and polish. There was a large kitchen, also many bedrooms. They slept in separate bedrooms.

The master's office was set apart from the main part of the house. Above the office there was a room, that was where Misha and I slept, "our room".

Braun's wealth came from a farm he owned, an assembly factory where mostly French and Belgians POWs worked. Their treatment there was not good. A couple of Poles or Ukrainian, French and Belgians also toiled on the farm. I as a servant in the house, my situation wasn't bad. I ate my meals with the POWs who worked there. I didn't meet any Russian POWs there.

My work started early in the morning. First I had to go to the house where I swept, tidied and polished and generally cleaned. As I finished these chores I would hear a bell tinkle, it was my signal, I was being summoned to the mistress's bedroom to help her dress and brush her hair. Oh how I hated that woman. Sometimes when brushing her hair I would tug her hair, winding some strands into the bristles and dragging the hair brush in anger.

When she had her lady guests' visit, I was given the position of serving them with snacks. I wore a white pinny and a white frilly band on the top of my head and would push a trolley with food from the kitchen to the guests in the dining or sitting room. On one occasion I was busy cleaning the kitchen after the food had been prepared, when I was ordered to take the laden trolley to the guests. Quickly grabbing the small table on casters I made my way, forgetting to change into my clean, white uniform. Entering to serve the ladies with my dirty cleaning clothes, they started averting their eyes away from me.

In bounced the plump mistress, red faced. She grabbed me dragging me into the kitchen. Fortunately I just received a tongue lashing as there were other servants in the kitchen. Also there were her guests, she didn't want to cause too much of a fuss.

She was the type of woman who would have her eyes darting about to make sure no one took a crumb without her knowledge. When de-stoning cherries for pies or if we were shelling peas, not one was allowed to be eaten. I would wait until she had to turn away and then would pop the cherries or peas into my mouth. The mistress was stupid. On a morning she would have collected windfall apples and pears so that no servant could get and eat any of the fruit. I would wait until an opportunity would arise for me to go by the fruit trees. I would pluck any fruit I desired off the branches and hide them. In the evening as I headed back to our room over the office I would retrieve them for me and Misha to enjoy.

It was hard work, but not too bad. Someone came to wash the windows, of which there were many. A woman was there for the laundry, but I was on my own having to clean the house, help in the kitchen, serve when needed and other chores. I was pregnant with Lida, but after surviving the factory, camp and prisons this was a decent life. But always the fear, gnawing away at you, what will tomorrow bring.

The mansion where we were was not far from Cologne. The bombing raids on the city were becoming regular, lighting the night skies that could be seen in the distance. Then we would get under cover. It was the early part of the day, off I went to the house to begin my work in the kitchen. The other servants hadn't arrived yet so I was on my own. Feeling hungry I noticed a loaf of bread on the kitchen table. Knowing I would not get anything to eat and would have to wait for dinner to be served in the yard before my hunger was fed; I cut myself a piece of bread. The bell rang; I went to help her dress. After doing my usual routine and brushing her hair she told me that I could go. So descending the stairs I made my way back into the kitchen with Frau Braun following not far behind. A couple of minutes after entering the kitchen she noticed a piece of bread had been cut from the loaf. She went berserk shouting "you've stolen bread" she started walking towards me. I was younger, stronger than the small dumpy woman who was threatening me.

She came closer to me. With all the strength I had, I grabbed hold of her shoulders and began shaking her, swearing at her in Russian. I shook her until I'd weakened my arms. The realisation came to me. What am I doing, what if she had a heart attack. Only the two of us in the house, as it was early morning and the other workers hadn't arrived yet. Her husband was out hunting, the son away in the army. Oh no I thought, that will be the end of me. I let go of her and she ran to the phone. Picking up the receiver she spoke to someone. Being quick thinking and cunning, as she finished her call I scratched my face with my nails, they were sharp, tussled my hair and clothes so that it appeared that she had attacked me.

A little later on in walked her foreman and his wife, who was a sturdy woman. Just looking at her put me in fear. If she had decided to shake me, all my teeth and bones would have rattled and dropped out. Behind them they had brought my husband. The mistress began to wail. "She's attacked me; she's been swearing and hitting me." Looking dejected in a calm, quiet voice I said "I didn't touch you, look what a state I'm in, by you assaulting me. I was only defending myself." My husband defended me by saying "my wife wouldn't do such a thing, she's a good woman."

The millionaire's wife Frau Braun was a nasty woman. No local German wanted to work for her so only foreign labour, that had no choice, were sent to her.

Being away hunting, of course Mr Braun was not present. The foreman believed me I think, because he said we'd wait until the master's return. Gradually the situation calmed down. When the master arrived home there was no mention of the incident.

The day arrived when their son came home on leave. In stature he was small, similar height to his mother. He was a handsome man with a kind nature. He had been at the battle front in the Ukraine, had seen and experienced the cruelty of war. He spoke a little Ukrainian and I German, of course. I also knew how to "behave" with people; I used my wits, so we got on alright, having short conversations if we met.

One evening the Brauns had been entertaining. After the guests had left I had the task of washing the plates, dishes etc, that had been in use, finishing the dishes, I began washing the glasses. The wine glasses were good quality, expensive, but more important than the price of them was that they had previously belonged to her mother.

Having finished rinsing the glasses, I picked a teacloth up to start drying them. As I got hold of the first glass, somehow, I don't know how, as I was being careful, the glass slipped out of my hand, smashing on the hard kitchen floor. The son was standing nearby, quick as a flash he stepped near to the pieces of shattered glass. Mrs Braun came over, dashing across the kitchen, old squat, waddling like a duck.

He picked up a piece of glass, looking at his mother he said, "It was me mother, I caught it with my sleeve." At hearing that remark she calmed down. He smiled at me, then walked away. Many a time he would defend me, but he wasn't at home long, his leave ended and he had to rejoin his army unit.

Mrs Braun carried keys, always having them on her person, making sure all the cupboards and larders were locked. One time she unlocked a cupboard and popped out of the kitchen. Quickly I took my chance. I grabbed a handful of choc/nuts out of a jar, shoving them into my bosom. She came back a moment later to lock the door, but I had got my prize.

Going upstairs to clean the bedrooms and change the bed linen, putting my hand into my bosom, I pulled out a nut and popped it to my mouth. I discovered the "nut/choc" was a coffee bean which was of no use to me, so collecting my "nuts" from my bra I threw them through a window into the ivy that was growing up the house. (The coffee was "Bona Kaffe" which was rare and expensive at that time).

Days went by with no particular incidents. The Bauers, who had POWs in the assembly factory, also had POWs working on their farm. Treatment of them was not good, their food being delivered from somewhere else. I don't know why but they were not allowed to speak to anyone outside their group.

When the owner/master was at home he didn't speak to me, he wasn't interested in chit chat. He gave me my orders of what jobs he wanted me to do, that was all. An elderly man, large built, a tall man. One day he called me into his office, he was sat behind his desk. Looking up at me he said, "Frau Teclik, I'm going to have to send you to the "Arbizam"? (The office where the labour force was controlled from). "Your husband" he continued, "has run away and I need workers." It was a long time later I was to discover why Misha had absconded.

The reason being, he had lost the keys to the office. There were two keys to the office, Bauer had one and as our room was above the office we had the other key so that we could get to our room. Having lost the key he panicked, expecting a beating he ran off, deciding to make his way to

Bonn, the town that was near the Rhine. As he made his way he started to get tired so decided to have a rest. The fool! Instead of sitting out of sight, he lay down on the bank of the river where he dropped to sleep.

A passing policeman saw him as it was a workday most of the populous were at work so it was even more noticeable that a man was laying snoozing on the grassy bank. The policeman approached Misha who was unaware of the situation as he was dozing. Waking him up the policeman enquired who was he and where was he from. Of course it was obvious he was a foreign worker on the run, so Misha was taken to the police headquarters.

A phone call was made to the farmer who was in charge of Bauer's farm. The police were told that Misha was sabotaging the workforce, not working himself and stopping others from working, so no! they didn't want him back. For this report from Mr Bauer and Co. Misha was put into a solitary confinement cell in prison.

Here the events that had happened parted us from one another, I had to go another way.

The master came to me and said, "Collect your belongings, you have to go to Abizan? (labour office). With tears in my eyes I put my meagre possessions into a bundle, thoughts were racing through my head. "I'm pregnant! What's going to happen to me? Misha isn't here, maybe he's been killed – shot." Don't forget at that time I had no idea what had become of him, it was a long time after when I received information about my husband.

I was given my documents and off I went to the labour office. That day was cold with a drizzle in the air as I made my way with my bundle to find out where I would be sent to next. Would it be a factory, a farm? Maybe a servant again? Not being bad looking with blond hair I suited the German taste of a maid, and I had knowledge of the German language.

Chapter Eighteen

The One Legged Nazi

The next place of work was given to me it was at Muhoo? I don't know, I can't remember everything after forty six years have passed! My documents were given to me along with my instructions of how to reach the place. Because I spoke the German language, I was given permission to travel by train to my destination. The views were lovely. Not far down the line I reached the railway station where I had to get off.

Waiting for me was the mistress of the house. As she could drive she had come to pick me up in her car. Looking through the window of the car, it was pleasant to gaze at the beautiful German countryside as we drove down the narrow lanes. Trees, fields, orchards, then steppes and forests. Houses dotted here and there. It appeared peaceful, no sounds of bombings or factory hooters. Planes droning above could be heard or maybe a train's whistle letting you know it was passing by.

The place I arrived at consisted of a shop, a restaurant and a small dairy farm, which had four or six cows. I don't remember how many but I do remember French POWs came to milk the cows. The dairy was for the use of the family.

The owner of this estate, or properties would be more correct, was an important commander on the front. He came from a large wealthy family from Westerwold/Betsvalü? Where his father owned a factory, but this prosperous enterprise belonged to his son, the commander.

As the commander was away the responsibility of running the place was left to his wife, his sister and her husband. The husband, the commander's brother-in-law was a true Nazi. He was always dressed in his dark mustardy coloured uniform, strutting about. Strutting not really being the correct word, because he had a pronounced limp. He only had one leg, the other leg was wooden. I don't know how or where he had lost his leg, maybe that's why he was such a disagreeable individual? A spiteful man.

The local estate owners and farmers disliked him. They had foreign workforces who worked on their land, Poles, Ukrainians etc. The reason for their hostility was that their one legged neighbour would watch everyone's movement, reporting to the police any incidents, arresting workers. He thought he had the right as he was a Nazi.

Now returning back to the farm.

The house was a substantial building, where the commander's sister and her Nazi husband with their four children lived. Also of course the commander's wife – they had no offspring.

There were large outbuildings where the cows and horses were housed. The place I was to sleep was a stable where there were only horses and hay. It was at the far end of the building. I was given a blanket to make myself a bed on the straw.

My work was varied, I had chores in the house cleaning, washing, ironing, pealing potatoes, preparing vegetables, polishing shoes, general housework. Also as it was late summer, one of my jobs outside was to make sheaves out of the corn. Although I slept in the stable on the straw, it was not too bad, the food was decent and it was quite peaceful.

Bombs could be heard but at a distance, where they were being dropped on large towns. Or you would hear the droning of engines as the planes flew overhead. Looking up eyes would follow their path as they flew onwards, over woods and fields. Death on its way to find its quarry.

As I watched my heart would sink. "How many bombs will be dropped, how many tears will be shed?" Always on my mind the children, the innocents, remembering how my brothers and sister had suffered. Nazi fascists! There were plenty. However ordinary German workers suffered also, unlike the wealthy, who had the choice of fleeing to their homes in the countryside away from danger. Ordinary people, the workers in factories and towns, the man and woman on the street experienced shortages and fear but they had nowhere to run to.

The commander's spouse and his sister started fraternising with the French. When the Nazi husband went to his job at the factory and the children to school, they would start making merry, eating, drinking, and fornicating with the French workers. Once walking into the barn I saw the sister in a passionate embrace in the hay with a Frenchman. I retreated at speed.

She of course was afraid of her husband. They both knew if he suspected or knew of their dalliances with the French he would report to the commander, his brother-in-law, but the women were decent with me. It was none of my business, certainly not in my interest to "see" or "notice" their antics.

Now I'll return to Misha.

When he ran off and was caught he was locked up in a solitary cell but somehow managed to pass a note to a Ukrainian man who was being released. Apparently Misha and the liberated Ukrainian had common acquaintances, who then passed the note to some friends of ours, who let me know where he was. This was, maybe after a couple of months how I discovered that my husband was in prison.

A short time later the commander returned from the front. He was a bigwig, an important man. His uniform was covered with braids and decorations, a cross (Iron Cross?) hung on his uniform. I waited a few days, building up the courage to approach him about my problem. I knew if I gave birth and there was no father for the child the baby would be taken away from me. As we were forced labour we would have to share looking after the child, if I was on my own how could I work?

Eventually I asked to speak to him. He wasn't a bad man; though he'd fought at the front he was decent enough with me. As I started to explain my situation, he sat patiently listening. My husband was in prison, I had recently found out about it. He was accused of being a saboteur, but he was not! I continued nervously. My husband's father had been an officer in the Austro-Hungarian army. Although he was Polish, my great grandparents were also nicknamed Aaustriti as they had originated from the part of Ukraine that had been under the Austro-Hungarian rule.

Also telling him the truth about our imprisonment and how we had run away from the factory. All this I told him with tears in my eyes. Those tears must have moved him, as I stood before him obviously pregnant. He decided he would help me.

The next day arrived. I was told to go to the front of the house and wait. A motorbike and sidecar were outside, near the front door. The commander followed me out and told me to get into the sidecar then off he drove, taking me to the Burgermaster's office.

There he explained to the Burgermaster my situation giving him the information in a long letter. That Misha was not a saboteur and his father had been an Austrian officer, which was part true, but he was Polish, maybe Ukrainian (God knows) but his grandfather had, or previously owned factories in Lvov (West Ukraine). I'll tell you about that later.

After the Burgermaster had read the letter, he and the commander agreed to give me permission to visit my husband in Bonn where he was in prison. I was handed a pass and the letter that had been written by the commander. With this and the Burgermaster's signature, it was relatively safe for me to travel. Early Sunday morning I collected my documents, ready to start my search for Misha.

One of the German employees drove me to the rail station by car, where I was put on the train, destination Bonn. The night previous, Bonn had suffered heavy bombing raids, and on my arrival there it was evident from the scenes of destruction. The air was hazy from the debris, dust hovering in the air. (Bonn was to become the headquarters of the government officers of West Germany after the war).

The river Rhine ran through the centre of Bonn dividing the city into two sections. One section being Bonn, the other section was known as Boyle. Because I spoke the German language I could ask for directions as to where to find the prison where my husband was confined.

Seeing the prison gates looming ahead I made my way towards them. It was difficult to get through as there was rubble and stones everywhere from the bombings. Eventually I came across a path that had been cleared of the stones and bricks which led to the gates. Arriving at the entrance

I rang a bell and waited, in a while a policeman came. I handed him the letter and he let me enter inside, closing the gates behind me.

These events were only made possible because of the actions of the commander. Also because I was quick witted enough to tell them that Misha's father was an Austrian officer, even though by nationality he was Polish. If I hadn't thought of telling them that, Mishka would certainly have been a goner for being accused of sabotage. If you were Ukrainian there was a chance of clemency. If you admitted to being Russian there was no chance of survival. Whether POW or civilian, at that time, in Germany to be a Russian was a death sentence, you were a "swine astrabieter."

After reading the letter he went into the sentry box and phoned into the prison. Turning to me he said, "Spreche sie Deutsch", (Do you speak German?), "Ya" I replied. "Herr Teclik, spreche Deutsch?" "Ya" again I answered. I felt nervous as I was escorted down a corridor. Entering a room where wooden tables with wooden benches stood, (*maybe a dining room?), I was told to sit and wait.

When Mishka heard his name called out, he was very frightened. This being Sunday he thought he was being taken out to be shot, poor thing.

Mama cries recalling this scene.

I sat waiting. Some time had passed, and then the door opened and in walked my husband. I could hardly recognise him. He was so thin, his hair had grown long and he was unshaven. He had been in solitary confinement "odinochka" for 6 weeks. What does it mean? It means you are on your own, no sounds, silence, for weeks. To experience this a prisoner could go out of his or her mind. As I've previously told you, I spent time on my own in a cell in Nuremberg so I understand a little, but I had got the airmen, who kept my morale up. To sit in silence, windows, doors closed, only being let out to empty the bucket on a morning. Let God protect anyone in such a situation.

Misha stood there, his dark hair lank and long, his blue eyes looked at me anxiously. "Katya", he said, tears running down his face, "Have you been arrested? What have you done? Have they arrested you?". "No!" I replied, "I'm not arrested, I've been allowed to visit you." Starting to get distraught, "What on earth have you done, why did you run away, why?

You know I was pregnant". I started to weep. "You knew the baby would be taken away from me if it had no father."

"I was afraid" he answered. "The master was going to beat me". "Better that he beat you!" I cried. It would have passed, we could have still been together on that farm, you could have endured suffered like I've had to, but you left, leaving me to face the misery on my own". He was weeping. "I was so afraid" he whispered. "Misha you left me on my own, why didn't you face up to the beating?" I said angrily. Though angry, pity for him soon took over my emotions.

The letters I had taken that had been written and signed by the Burgermaster and the commander made life easier for him. After I left, that same day he was transferred from a solitary cell to a general cell where the treatment and conditions were an improvement for him.

As I made my way back to the place I had come from I felt happy that the commander had kept his word and had helped me. Happy and relieved that I had found Misha. On my return back to the farm I thanked him, for I was grateful to him for his help, he was good to me, didn't insult or beat me. Now and again he showed an interest in the Ukraine and would question me on different aspects of life in my homeland.

He was home on leave, maybe two or three weeks. During this time his parents came to stay, also family and friends. It was a bustling time as there were banquets and parties held regularly for him.

The day of his departure arrived. His family were all gathered to wave him off, back to the fighting. Before leaving he had said to me, "Well when we take the Ukraine, then you'll be able to go there." I thought to myself. "I've experienced your taking of my homeland," but said nothing. You have to understand the situation I was in; I had to bite my tongue. Off he went on his way back to the front.

Well life continued as before. The two ladies continued their dalliance with the French. My life was comfortable – but – him without the leg was a nasty man with me very nasty. In fact his own wife and children feared him; he was so severe and cruel. He took his spiteful anger out on people because he'd lost his leg. I don't know where he'd lost it, at the front or somewhere else, but the result was his wooden limb.

As I said previously, life was not harsh for me at this place. Some evenings after our work had finished, young men and young women would meet up gathering together chatting about their day, their homes, loved ones, sometimes even managing to joke. But as I kept finding out, nothing good lasted for me, something always turns up.

It had been a lovely day with the sun shining on us all day as we cut the wheat, binding it into golden sheaves. We had been working in the fields from early morning with a short break at midday. Finishing our reaping and binding of sheaves we came out of the field, making our way back to the yard for something to eat and rest. The Nazi was stood waiting for us. As I was about to pass him, he stopped me. "You! Go and polish the floors upstairs" he snarled. The floors were wooden and varnished or painted, with rugs placed on top and arranged about the rooms. This was seven maybe seven thirty in the evening but he was preparing for the next day as he was expecting friends from town as guests.

I'm hungry! I answered. "I've been in the fields all day." "Go and polish the floors now!" he shouted. "Then maybe you'll get something to eat." "No!" I stood my ground, refusing to obey him. The house was a large building with wide stairs that led to a landing that had many rooms leading off it. On one side of the large house was a restaurant (bar) on the other side of the house was a shop. When the shop was closed after a day's trading, then the restaurant (bar) would be ready for the evening, where the local farmers and gentlemen could go for a drink and company.

"No!" I screeched "Not until I've had something to eat!" He grabbed hold of me and started pulling me by my sleeve up the stairs. I stubbornly refused to go and tried breaking away from his grip. These events were taking place about eight o clock in the evening, maybe a little later. The restaurant had started to fill up with the farmers and gentry who no doubt could hear the rumpus from the house.

He started pulling me, pushing me. We had reached the top of the stairs. I don't know what happened next, whether it was the way I had struggled away from him or had I pushed him, but the next thing he had lost his balance. Trah, trah, trah as he went flying down the stairs, then he was at the bottom laying still, unmoving. If he was dead then I would have the charge of murder brought against me.

Fear and panic took me over. "Oh God! What have I done? I'll be arrested and shot". The feeling of dread gave my feet wings. Running down the wide staircase I jumped over the motionless figure. Where could I run? Where could I hide? Making a dash for the stable that was my temporary home; I closed and barred the doors.

I will never know how I didn't miscarry with the events.

Meanwhile a doctor had been sent for. My tormentor had only been stunned. He was laid in his bed as his wooden leg had been broken in the fall. I wasn't afraid that he would chase me, as he couldn't on one leg. He couldn't do anything until his leg was repaired.

Laying down on my bed of hay, I started crying bitterly, praying to God. "Help me, what can I do?" I can't describe the feeling of fear that came over me. I had a picture in my mind. I was being arrested, I was being hanged, I was being shot. Those images would not go away and every time I heard a sound, I trembled, convinced that they had come for me. Come to take me away.

Fate of the one legged Nazi

This is what I heard. After the war just as the front had passed, a group of men came to the house, they told the wife and his four children to go upstairs. The Nazi was led down to the cellar where wine/beer barrels were stored and shot him dead. Who these men were I don't know, it could have been his foreign workers, or it could even have been his German neighbours as he was despised by them for having some of them arrested. He was bad!

Back to my story.

Night was approaching and still no one came. Maybe because he was stunned, laid in bed, probably not remembering what had happened, as the fall had been a bad one.

I remained in the stable behind the barred doors. As the doors were closed the unpleasant smell of the horse soiled hay was getting stronger as it had not been cleaned out, so no fresh hay had been put down, but that was the least of my worries.

The same thoughts kept repeating themselves in my head. "I have to run away, what will happen to me if I do? Where do I run to? How do I make my escape?" It was quiet in the stable; still every little sound startled me. After much deliberation I made my decision. To go at night was a foolhardy thing to do as I was nervous of travelling at night in my pregnant condition. The train station was five or six miles away, also public rail did not run at night. If I managed to get there before the trains started running, I was aware I would be noticeable, risking following my husband's fate, dawn was the time I'd start my journey.

I began gathering my meagre possessions together, making a bundle, then I lay down to rest and await daybreak. A while later, maybe the middle of the night or thereabout, I heard a tapping on the door. Going closer to the doors I heard a murmuring of voices. As I listened I recognised who it was. The voices belonged to two Ukrainian labourers who worked on a nearby farm.

Stacik was the name of one; I've forgotten the other man's name. Stacik came from Ivan Frankivsk. During conversations we'd had I mentioned that my grandparents had once lived there, before heading east during the First World War, he always called me zemlyachka (fellow country woman).

Tapping on the door, Stacik said, "Katya open the door, it's us," "no" I answered nervously, "Maybe someone has sent you," "Katya don't be afraid, we won't harm you." They started telling me why they were knocking on my door at this late hour.

Apparently, the incident that I had been involved in had been heard and witnessed by some of the patrons that were going to the restaurant bar. One man, a farmer, on his arrival home must have been mulling over the events of the evening, and what could happen to me, as on his return he went to his Ukrainian labourers.

Briefly explaining what had happened, then saying to them, "Lads you have to help her to escape. Early morning take her to the station, let her flee to wherever she can" he continued, "because he is a vindictive man. When he recovers and gets his leg back, she will be handed over to the Gestapo. It's even possible he could kill her himself. Nothing would be said or done as he has close links with the Gestapo." After hearing what they had told me, and hoping it was true not just a story to make me open the door, I decided I had to trust them and slid the bars off.

Opening the door I let the lads enter. They were well looked after by their farmer. With them they had brought some provisions for me, cucumber, tomatoes, bread, also some type of salami. Their master must have been a kind hearted man as he had given them documentation passes, so if we were stopped we could prove we were on a genuine errand. With them they had two bicycles, and just before daybreak I picked up my bundle and off we rode, me with Stacik and the other lad on his bicycle riding with us in charge of my scanty belongs.

Chapter Nineteen

Camp Troisdorf
Dynamit-Actien-Gesellschaft – 9.9.43 – 7.2.45

It was a pleasant journey down the country lane, there was a slight frost on the ground, and the sun had just started to rise. Birds were beginning their morning chorus as we rode past fields, woods and valleys with rivers running through them.

If I had been travelling this path in freedom, it would have been joyful, but on my mind and in my heart were the fearful thoughts. What's going to happen to me? What's going to be my fate? What will happen to my baby? Where and what awaits me? Praying to God to help me.

After our ride of five or six miles we arrived at the railway station. The trains had started running, taking people from the countryside to their jobs in town. Parting from my saviours I joined the early morning crowd and got on the train. I found a seat and waited impatiently for the train's whistle, the signal that the train was ready to go, taking me further away from the events that would have caused me grief.

The train was passing through Siegburg which was the nearest town to where I'd boarded. I had decided what I was going to do. Arriving in Siegburg I got off. Getting out of the carriage, I made my way out of the station and headed for the Aberzam (labour control).

Arriving at the Aberzam I entered, the staff that were employed there were elderly, decent people. This place covered the labour force for a large area. One of the staff looked at me and started chuckling. "Vas Mahstun?" "What have you done?" he asked me three times "Vas Mahstun? What have you been up to?" "I haven't done anything" I replied. "No! You never do anything. This is the fourth time we've seen you," he glanced down at some papers that were on his desk and continued. "Running away from the factory – you didn't do anything. At the restaurant, you were sent to – you didn't do anything?" I listened to him, trying to work out what I was going to say when I was given a chance to explain what had occurred and why I was here.

His voice went on, "after the restaurant had sent you here, you were sent to Herr Becks. According to you, you didn't do anything wrong. Now again at Herr "so and so's" place you are blameless, done nothing wrong."

I started to give my account of the events that had taken place. "As you can see I'm pregnant, I had been working in the fields all day. It was evening, maybe seven o'clock, all I did was to ask him for something to eat as I was feeling sick and faint, he refused. I was going to clean the room, when he grabbed hold of me and started dragging me towards his room.

I didn't know what he wanted from me, as he was always touching me and nipping my bottom. I was frightened that he wanted me, wanted to sleep with me, rape me, that's why I was being dragged to his bedroom. I started to struggle, trying to get out of his grasp, when he stumbled on his wooden leg. He had tripped himself up and went hurtling down stairs. I'm not to blame!" I carried on telling my tale of what had happened. "I got frightened knowing that I would get the blame, be accused of pushing him. I had to run away. I came here to you. I could have kept going, getting farther away, but I didn't. I came here to report what had happened."

They looked at one another, then one of the staff went away. I waited. In a short while he returned. "Spreche sie Deutsch?" "Do you speak German?" "Ya" I answered. "Can you write in German? Can you read in German?" My answer was "yes" to all the questions. "We're going to send you as an interpreter to a factory not far away here at Troisdorf." It was maybe five kilometres away. Of course I wasn't being sent as a head or main interpreter, but to assist, as the camp was large.

I was given documents and passes to get to my next place of work, off I went to the tram stop. Getting on the tram I soon arrived in Troisdorf and went in search of the camp. As I approached there was a factory on top of a hill. On one side of the factory were forests as far as the eye could see, but I was to find out beneath those endless trees, under the forest was an underground factory. I'd heard that it stretched five kilometres.

Here under the earth of the forest, rockets, bombs, God only knows what other armaments of destruction were being manufactured. The factory on top of the hill was where the ammunitions were made. It was called "Dynamite Factory." There was high security everywhere round the factory and its underground extension.

On the other side of the factory were the labour camps, where a thousand or more female workers were housed in barracks. Row upon row of these wooden structures, maybe seventy women in each one. Mixed nationalities were in the labour force that the camp was for. Serbs, Croats, Russian, Ukrainians but mostly "our people" Soviet/East Ukrainians.

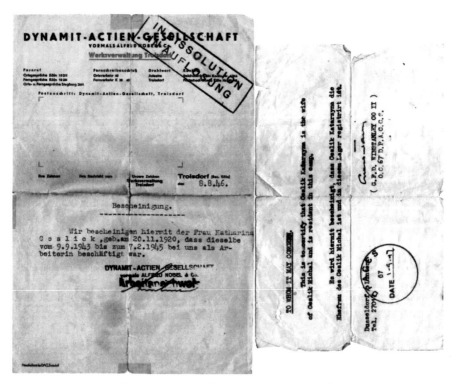

Evidence of forced labour in Alfred Nobel & Co.

As I said previously, the camp was very large, and was divided into different sections. Next to our work camp, behind the wire fence, were the French girls. Further again there was a wire barrier, and in between were Italian POWs, I think. I think about 2000 girls in total.

Now I'm going to tell you about "Camp Troisdorf"

Troisdorf was a small place which consisted of a couple of streets. The rest of the area was where the factories and camps were. On one side of the labour camps were the railways, where the manufactured weapons of destruction were loaded on to wagons, to be transported to their destination. A destination that would end in death and devastation.

Troisdorf factories must have been on a map, as I was to find out. The place was bombarded on a regular basis. The bombs would hit the railways and the forests but did little damage to the underground industry. It was as if the attacking airmen knew where the labour camps were, where innocent people were, because to my knowledge the bombs never hit the worker's barracks.

When the siren sounded all the police/guards would run to hide in their bunkers. That was when we had the chance to make our escape, but it wasn't that simple. There were guard dogs and though sometimes the wire fence had fallen with the blasts, where would we run to? Where?

Arriving at the camp I looked at the entrance. Oh! Oh! It's not what I imagined it would be. Two soldiers were guarding the entry. The camp was very long and wide, full of those barracks. I showed them my documentation, they pointed to a bureau where I was to go for my instructions. At the office again I gave them my papers. After reading the information that was written on them they sent me to the department of Vengela and Fritz. Every police guard had a quota of barracks under their control.

Arriving at Vengela and Fritz's office I entered and was met by a young man. I say young, he was maybe forty. He wore a black uniform with the red and yellow kroytz (swastika?) armband; he was missing one limb, his arm. The uniform he wore indicated he belonged to the SS or one of their divisions. His arm had been lost in battle, he was a brutal man, everyone was afraid of him, even the Commandant appeared uneasy in his presence.

In general the post of Commandant was given to elderly Germans to run the work camps. The Commandant at our Troisdorf camp was a decent man, tall with a moustache, he never beat anyone nor did them harm. It was the underlings; they were the ones who dished out their cruel acts on the workers, usually behind the Commandant's back.

Mostly the police guards who were under the commander's control were the ones who couldn't go to the front because of war injuries and disabilities, or other reasons that prevented them from frontline battle. At Vengela's office I was shown into a small room with a bed in the corner. This is where I would be sleeping. I was to be an assistant to the senior interpreter. *(September 1943?)*

I started my work. When I met the girls in the barracks, they looked at me and started laughing, "Ha, ha, ha" they started to make fun of me. "So some Frenchy has already put his mark on you." I was always small and slim but my tummy was rounded, it was obvious I was pregnant. I couldn't hide the evidence. "No!" I replied, no Frenchman or Belgian has done anything to me, I have a husband who's in prison for trying to escape." "Oh yes," they jeered not believing what I had told them. I started my duties as an interpreter.

We rose out of bed early in the morning; a small slice of bread, so thin, as if it was gauze that you could see through, was given to us. This was our breakfast. At dinner time we went to the canteen where we were mostly given soup (gruel). Let me tell you about the soup, and how careful you had to eat it, or your teeth could break. The soup was very watery, pieces of turnip peel, potato peel, pieces of very crunchy potatoes floating in it, similar to potato crisps of today only harder. You may think – well that's not too bad. The problem was as you crunched your way through the soup you could get pieces of string, sand and even glass was found at times.

One morning I started work. I had to report to Vengela to be told what she wanted me to do. I had to follow the orders of Vengela or Fritz. "Frau Teclik! Go to Barrack numbers ….. Tell them their beds must be made, the floors scrubbed everything in order as we are going to inspect their room."

Off I went heading to the barrack, entering and calling our, "Girls! Vengela has sent me to tell you to put your room in order". They started complaining. I continued "you have to make your beds, clean the floors, there's going to be an inspection." Insults started to be hurled at me. "You bitch! you're not telling us what to do, you cow!" Leaving the barracks with their foul language still ringing in my ears, trying to find a place to hide, so my tears would not be seen by Vengela. If she had seen me crying she would have tried to discover the reason I was weeping. Then there would have been trouble for the girls.

Life would have been easier for me if I had twisted the truth, or if I had been an informer or traitor and just thought of my own comfort. With my knowledge of the German language I could have lied and said that I had Austrian lineage or was of German decent. "I'm Russian" I would say, "a Soviet". Educated in the USSR there was no difference between Russian/Ukrainian, both the same as far as I was concerned. I stayed devoted to my motherland.

When West Ukrainians or Polish Ukrainians as they were known, tried to tell me I was Ukrainian, "No I'm Russian" I would answer. It was later when I got to understand that I'm a Ukrainian and I'm from Ukrainian descendants, but in those days to me a Soviet Ukrainian or Russian were the same family, the same nation. I was a Soviet, Russian, Ukrainian, no difference to me.

- West Ukraine up to 1772 was under Polish reign.
- In 1772 it came under the power of Austria.
- From 1867 Austro-Hungarian Empire.
- In October 1918 the Austro-Hungarian Empire collapsed. Western Ukrainian Peoples Republic (ZUNR) was proclaimed, but in the summer of 1919 the Western Ukraine was annexed by Poland.
- September 1939 division of Poland by Berlin and Moscow, West Ukraine became a part of USSR.
- From 1941 until 1944 under Nazi occupation.
- From 1944 the Western Ukraine together with the rest of Ukraine was part of the USSR until August 1991.

Many a time I was given instructions to relay a message but didn't go, I was afraid of being beaten by the girls, as they were forever abusing and cursing me. I couldn't cause them any trouble by denouncing them; I had witnessed the repercussions of such behaviour during my enforced journey across Germany.

If I had reported to Vengela that Barrack No 5 won't listen to me, won't listen to the instructions, then they would have all been punished severely, possibly be sent to a concentration camp, depending on what mood she was in. Fritz wasn't as malicious when compared to Vengela, she was unmarried a spinster, a very bitter angry woman.

I couldn't tolerate the situation, so decided to wait until the time Vengela was not on duty, as I then wouldn't have to ask for her permission to go and see the Commandant of the camp. It was the policewoman Vengela's day off, taking the opportunity of her absence, I made my way to the head man's office.

Agreeing to see me he asked me what my problem was. Bursting into tears I tried to explain that I needed his permission for a transfer to work in the factory. "Why?" he asked. "I'm pregnant and finding the situation difficult, the girls are my country women, I can't tell them what to do," I answered. Agreeing with my transfer he gave me the authorisation to start work at the factory.

A sense of happy relief came over me. I had disentangled myself from such an awkward predicament of being laughed at, ridiculed and sworn at, now life would be a little easier.

It was not far from the camp to the factory, everything was in walking distance. The road that led to the factory was a mile, maybe a little longer. A forest bordered one side of the road and the camps lined the other side. Also on the right hand side of the road was a street with a row of houses where some German people lived. So if there were any thoughts of doing a bunk, there was no where to escape, no where to run.

I was returning from my first day at the factory, it was the morning shift that had just ended and I was making my way back to my quarters. Vengela had returned to her post. She marched in and started giving me instruction, "Frau Teslik!" she barked. "Go and tell barrack number

4 to prepare for inspection." When she had finished giving me my instructions I looked at her answering, "I don't work for you anymore. I'm not an interpreter." "Whose told you this?" her voice had risen a pitch. "The Commandant, I went and asked for his permission to work at the factory" I answered. "The Commandant sent me, I've just returned from my shift."

She started calling me names, screeching, "How dare you go to the Commandant without my permission, without asking me?" "If I'd ask you, you would have refused me," was my muttered answer back. Whether she heard me, I don't know, she turned and marched out. But a price would be paid by me for daring to cross her; she took a vindictive grudge against me from there on.

It was early autumn, leaves had started to fall. After working my shift in the factory and walking back to the camp, Vengela was waiting for me with orders that the leaves had all to be swept up; so I would spend a few hours more sweeping. As autumn leaves had stopped dropping, then the winter snows started falling. My orders then were, after returning from the factory, to start clearing the roads and paths digging the snow away. It felt as if it was impossible to bear this burden, but I endured with the help of God and prayers, I survived.

During the time that I worked at the dynamite factory I got acquainted with a group of girls who, on their way home from work, had found a way of earning extra rations by doing chores, cleaning, ironing and washing for the German fraus, whose homes they passed on their way back to the barracks. In return for these tasks, they were given bread, sugar etc which was very handy in supplementing our diet or using the goods to barter with for what was classed as luxury items, chocolate, cigarettes etc.

Fate dealt me a lucky card, and gave me the good fortune of finding a very, very nice German lady who wanted some help running her home. Her husband had been killed at the front so on my way back from the factory I would call at her house to see if she needed any help. Sometimes I would glimpse a man skulking about, later I discovered it was the lady's brother who had come home from the front battle line and was in hiding, not wanting to return to the combat zone.

As time passed we got to know each other, understanding each other. She was a kind woman. I started to disclose my predicament to her, telling her that my husband was in prison and why. She understood what the consequences were, if the baby was born and no husband was on the scene, the baby would be taken away.

Again call it fate, luck or God's help, we started to chat. She asked me where my husband was, in which prison. To my amazement, apparently she had a brother who held a prominent position connected to the same prison where Misha was serving his sentence.

She contacted her brother explaining my predicament and asked him for his help. He agreed to try and get the official who was in charge of my husband's affairs to meet me. My champion applied for permission for me to visit the prison, making all the arrangements for the journey as she was going with me. The passes were for a Sunday, I remember as I was not at work.

Saturday night I curled my hair with rags, so my hair would look nice for my visit. The next morning I tried to make myself presentable. The choice of outfit wasn't difficult to decide on, my clothes consisted of a dress that now because of my condition didn't fit, a skirt and blouse with roses patterned on the material and a short waistcoat. The decision was made for me, the blouse and skirt it was.

There is a photo of mama in the skirt, blouse and waistcoat.

Though looking decent, there was not much I could do about my belly, not too big, still it protruded out in front of me.

It was late autumn, days were chilly and evenings were getting longer. After an uneventful journey we arrived at the prison in Bonn where my husband was confined. Entering the inspector's office I was told to sit down. He looked at me and started asking me questions in a mocking manner.

"Frau Teclik you do know what will happen to you when you have your child? You have no husband with you, so your child will be taken away from you," he taunted. "I know that" I answered him meekly. "That's why I'm here, to beg you to help me. Please, please can you help to get him released?" The interview lasted a long time; I've forgotten the details, though I wrote it down a few years ago, when my memory was fresher. I've lost the notes.

"Frau Teclik, you know very well that I have it in my power to send your husband to the concentration camp, or to release him," the man with my child's fate in his hands said. "But I can't let him go," he continued. You have both been in prison previously. He has had the accusation of being a saboteur against his name. Although this is doubtful, as we received letters from a Herr Braun refuting those allegation." He was silent for a moment, jotting something down on a writing pad he had before him on his desk.

Looking up he said, "I have sent many prisoners to the concentration camps, I don't know why, but I feel compassion towards you coming from Austrian Ukrainian predecessors. Also your husband's link (his father was an Austro Hungarian officer) you appear to be a good lass." He was silent then continued, "I can't discharge him now, I'm going to send him to Cologne to work for six weeks. When he has served his punishment, done his time, if he survives, I will try to have him sent to the camp where you are." His voice had a pleasant tone, almost friendly. Leaving the prison without managing to see Misha my German lady took me back home.

I carried on working for this kind lady. After finishing my shift in the factory I would go straight to her house to do any chores that needed doing, working honestly and diligently. In exchange for my cleaning, and doing the laundry etc, she would provide me with bread, sugar, butter, whatever she could spare, which was then taken gratefully to the camp. Life dragged on. To the factory, from the factory, calling at my German lady's house on the way back. One day was the same as before.

Maybe six weeks had past by since my visit to ask for Misha's release. Again my German lady's help was needed. She agreed and suggested that we get together some bits and pieces as small gifts for the "official" so he would be more inclined to give me permission to visit my husband. and take him some bread in his place of punishment in Cologne.

Our arrangements completed we made our way to the prison. On our arrival I was taken to the official's office. Walking in I smiled at him,

I was always brave, crafty in my life. I knew when a smile was needed, when to cry, when to keep my mouth shut and when to bow, keep my eyes downcast and subservient. Judging a situation, then behaving in a manner that would be useful to me. "Ya Frau Teslick, what is it you want?" he asked. Being nervous, wondering if he had any recollection of our conversation I started my somewhat weakly prepared speech.

"I've come to you, to ask for your permission to visit my husband, and take him some bread." He sat behind his desk looking at me as I continued. "I believe a German when he gives his word he will keep it. You promised me that after six weeks he would be released. Six weeks have past, I'm very frightened, and if anything happens to him I will lose my child. I don't want my baby taken away from me." He could see I was feeling upset.

I later found out that my concerns were valid. In our camp there were eleven babies born and only two survived, mine and another woman's the reason being that we escaped. As the war was coming to an end, the babies were taken to Siegburg, to a hospital or some place similar, where they were put to death. So nine women lost their babies, as we found out when we met some of them after the war.

"Yesterday I was in the camp in Cologne where he was sent." He said, "Your husband and a Yugoslav were brought back here and given documentation. We sent them to the labour distribution office in Siegburg; from there they were to be sent to your factory in Troisdorf." Though wanting this to be true, I did not know whether to believe him. We returned back and my German Frau headed home.

It was evening as I entered my barrack. I was met by the girls who shared my living quarters. "Katya, your husband has been here looking for you," one of them said. "He's working at a farm not far from here. My heart almost burst, it started beating fast with happiness. So it was true, the prison official had kept his word as he had promised and released my Misha. He had not been sent to the factory, but all that mattered to me was that he was near. The farm where he was had other young men and girls who laboured in the fields.

The next day after work, just as evening was falling I set off, clutching my permit and the address of the farm, to see my husband. He had just finished working. Looking up he saw me, the delight at seeing me lit up his face. He took me into his room; we kissed and embraced, both of us crying with happiness that my Mishinka had been released from imprisonment. We felt so much joy, so ecstatic that we were together again.

Happily we started meeting each other at the gates to the camp. If my working rota left me free in the evening I would ask for permission to see my husband. After being given my pass, I would eagerly hurry to the gate, where, after showing my permit and going through the exit, we would meet, not straying far from the fence. Just standing chatting about the day's events or what the future may hold for us. Sunday was a free day, so with authorisation I would go to the farm where he worked. These meetings carried on for two weeks, maybe three weeks, no longer.

One evening off I went to our usual place. No Misha. I waited a while but he didn't appear. Not that day, not the next day, or the day after. Sunday was my free day so I applied for a pass to go to the farm where he worked, but by chance the farm girls came to our factory camp. It was late Sunday morning. "Where's Misha," I asked them "why isn't he here?" "Oh he ran off a few days ago" one of the girls answered. "Oh God, again, now where do I search for him" I enquired. "There was something wrong with his leg the farmer wanted to lance it, so he skedaddled" one of the girls explained.

The following Sunday I went in search of him, deciding to start with the hospitals because of his leg. It was a risk to go anywhere without permission or a pass. With a pass you had to stay in the vicinity of the camp, not venturing more that 3 miles/5 kilometres from the camp. We couldn't travel by train or tram, but were free to wander within the 3 miles/5 kilometres boundary.

I headed for the hospital in Troisdorf; he wasn't there, as the hospital had no dealings with foreigners in the work camp. I took a risk and got on a tram to Siegburg, maybe he was in hospital there. So that's where I made my way. Arriving at the hospital barracks, I entered and enquired whether there was a Mihael Tieslick there. A sister told me yes he was there; she told me to follow her and led me to him. Walking into the ward I saw Misha sitting on the top of a two tier bed, his hair had been cut, his face shaven, he was wearing clean pyjamas and his leg was bandaged. "Misha, what happened now?" I exclaimed. Oh I did have a life with that man, I don't know! Maybe I was just born to suffer. He started to tell me why he'd run off. On his leg he had a large abscess. The farmer had wanted to lance it so he asked someone to hold Mishka down so the "master" could cut into the abscess. Mishka broke away, grabbed his boots and ran off. Catching the train he went to Siegburg barracks medical centre where he was cleaned up and his leg administered to.

Returning back to my "place", my next decision was to go and see the camp Commandant, to beg him to help Misha to work in the factory after he had left hospital. The Commandant listened to my request, and did everything he could to make it possible for Misha to be in our camp after his stay in hospital.

So, this was the state of affairs. My husband arrives at "my camp"; the camp authorities gave us a room together. It was situated a long way off from the gateways. I can see it as now, the barracks, then the small built bungalows, these housed the Foyks Deutch. Foyks Deutch were people who had one parent that was German and the other parent of another nationality. For example, maybe Germans that had been born in Russia, or as I said previously, one of the parents who were not German. Later these Foyks Deutch were allowed more freedom. Previous to them being put in the bungalows to stay, the bungalows were the domain of the camp police and staff.

The barracks where we were placed. As you entered on the right hand side there was the office of the police wardens, Vengela and Fritz. Facing the office on the left hand side was a larger room which housed an extended family, mother, father, children, and grandchildren. They all lived in one room, it was crowded as you can imagine. The main room of the barrack housed the toilets, and around the large room ran troughs for water, like you see in the fields for cows. Troughs built in cement around the edge; this was for water to get washed in. In the same main room there were bunk beds where seventy girls slept. Then at the end of the barracks was another room which was for two families to share. This was for me and Misha. The other couple were Valentine and his wife Ludmilla.

In our room there were two bunk beds, maybe three yards apart and two small cupboards, one for each family. A room opposite housed another couple. The husband was a chemist his name was Sikorski and his wife Marie. Also in their room was a Polish lady, she'd had a baby that had died because she could not produce milk to feed her infant. There was nothing else to feed her child with, nothing to give it so the poor mite died. *(I saved my baby by using my wit)*.

Aaah (sigh) so now a new chapter began in our lives.

Misha when he first came to the camp, was very good, and a very considerate husband. After all his suffering in prison he was so happy, so relieved to be out. He would wash the floor for me. I was heavily pregnant, he would bring me water and soup, help me when I washed our rags (clothes) There was no soap or hot water, so we used sand and a stone to try and scrub the clothes.

The room was infested with bugs, and the wooden beds that we slept in were full of the blood sucking insects. Of course when we got out of bed we were covered in bug bites. They used to spray us with DDT powder, both us and our beds, but there were so many of the bugs, the black insects, that it didn't make much difference. They crawled out of the wooden walls.

So right, I'm pregnant. When the planes flew overhead and the sirens sounded we would run to our shelters. I say shelters, they were trenches, always full of water at the bottom of these dug outs. These shelters were covered with wood and earth. The dug outs were more of a walk-in grave, ready made, for if a bomb dropped near and the earth trembled we would have been buried, as the structure appeared to be made for this to happen. Thank God that the bombs never hit the camp, though they fell on either side trying to hit the arms depot, the camp was never bombed until Christmas 1944.

Life in the camp at Troisdorf passed in this manner, for example, Misha worked from 6.00am to 6.00pm, I worked 6.00pm to 6.00am, this was alternated as our rota changed. Misha and I really didn't see each other, only maybe on a Sunday. The camp food was bad, beetroot, water, cabbage, water, sometimes potatoes in their skins. A couple of small pieces of bread, but we managed to get other food from the Germans that we did chores for on our way back from the factory. So that was our confinement in the labour camp.

Imagine, four men, all married and seventy young women, all in one barrack. When the men rose early to go to the toilet or to get washed, semi nude girls would be running around. They would have just got out of bed to prepare for the day and would also be getting washed and dashing to the same water trough and toilets. Like animals you could say. Ignore it, take no notice. But our men started to be not so nice, so we did take notice. **You have to remember it was 1940's and the morals were not as "enlightened" as in later years.**

There were too many girls about. In our section of the camp there were only eleven married couples and hundreds of young women. Along our camp, there were Polish and French camps, divided by barbed wire. Our girls were sneaky and would get pliers from their place of work, cut through the wires, making ways that they could secretly get through to the other sections, where there would be Belgian, French, Italian boyfriends to romance with.

In time my Misha started to stray, to wander, he was a handsome man, dark hair, blue eyes, a good singing voice and could play the guitar. Young, handsome, he was twenty three years of age in 1943, girls started to fall in love with him. The girls started bringing him spirits that were used to clean the machine in the factory. Now his problems **really** began.

In our room Misha had rigged up in secret an electric ring, which was under the bed out of sight. The spirits the girls brought was boiled, adding caramelised sugar, then it was used for drinking. Many people who drank this died or became blind. I never touched a drop. Cigarettes were another gift he was given. Amongst his admirers were two sisters, Nina and Zina. Nina the youngest sister fell in love with my Mishka, she was besotted with him. The sisters planned to kill me. After the war I met Nina again. She confessed that one night, her and her sister had been waiting for me, to arrange an accident as I was passing, but were interrupted. She was crying saying it was because she so wanted him, the other sister was making a play for him too.

The Russians (Soviets) in defiance to their "masters" were celebrating the October revolution. A group had gathered in the canteen, amongst them were the two sisters and my husband. As the concocted spirit flowed, the singing began. Revolutionary songs, folk songs, sad songs. As their celebration continued, the interpreter sat writing down the names of the participants that were revelling.

Misha came back to the barrack, he was drunk and he was hungry. We had been given soup, but he was still hungry. As I said it was made from beetroot or maybe cabbage and water. Sometimes you would get string, pieces of glass, grit in the soup. It had to be eaten carefully or teeth could be broken, eating that soup from the canteen. Well he came into our room, drunk, nasty as he always was in drink, I started to say something and he hit me, he beat me so hard I don't know what happened but I couldn't breathe. I lost my voice. How I didn't lose my baby I didn't understand. Off he went to another barrack where my friend lived. Also in the same barrack was another girl, one of Misha's admirers, she was a real beauty, this girls was always flittering (flirting) with Misha, kissing him, cuddling him.

Anyway off he went in his drunken state. When she saw him she started making advantages (advances) towards him. I'll leave it to your imagination, but he was in trouble again. The police came and he was locked up. I went to the police to beg for his release, frightened that if he was killed my baby would be taken away from me. The police released him but a short time later some others came and he was rearrested.

In this camp life could be very cruel. If the police or interpreter took a dislike to you, or you did something wrong, maybe get caught going through the wires to the boyfriend you were punished. The lasses didn't stop courting whether they were punished, hungry or beaten. They weren't deterred from getting to the affection at the other side of the wires.

Because I didn't work for Vengela she didn't leave me alone, still angry that I'd asked to work in the factory. On my return from work she always had some job waiting for me. Digging, sweeping, clearing leaves or snow. Because of my pregnancy I had a note from the doctor to be given lighter duties. No she didn't take any notice of that.

I'll tell you something of Michael. I loved him, he was a very clever man, it was the drink that made him nasty. When he was sober you couldn't ask for a better man.

Oh, what was I saying? Yes, about the punishment?

One of the penalties was to go and find "books" (bugs), not the ones you read, but the little black animals (insects) known as klopy in Russian, little black animals, bugs that climbed up the wall and into the wooden frame work of the barracks.

Mama's way of speaking English was funny at times, but no one dare laugh when she made an error, as she was self taught and very proud of her English language. If anyone made a remark she would answer "I speak better English than you speak my language!"

They were horrible, aaah! (shudder), they bit us terribly, feeding on our blood. These bugs had to be collected and put into a jar. When the jar was full, the next procedure was to stand in the centre of the room and squash them by hand, in between your fingers, with everyone watching. Aaah! it was horrible.

The barrack opposite our barrack was a place that always appeared to be having punishments metered out. Through my window, if I saw anyone being taken there, oooh! It goes through me just remembering. I saw a man being led by a black uniformed Nazi who had a false arm, with which the bastard kept beating his charge. Later he was brought out of the torture barrack, hardly able to walk, blood pouring down his face, and was taken to the prison that was in the camp. A scene I saw repeated many times through that window.

Life carried on, you just had to live. But still not bad, although long hours, hard work, bad food, bombings, it was better than the life I saw in prison.

Chapter Twenty

CHILDBIRTH

The time of my labour arrived. It was nightime when the terrible pain began. Michael was not there, as he had something wrong with his leg again, so was at the medical barrack. I stood up and water poured out of me, my waters had broken. Ludmilla, who we shared the room with, started rubbing my back, trying to comfort me. The police, two of them, Fritz and another one, who were on duty, just stood there and started to laugh. Organising the camp van, they bungled me into the back, telling the driver to take me to hospital. The driver didn't know that we weren't allowed in German hospitals. He drove me to the nearest one; it was five miles away I think. All the way I kept pushing back; frightened that she would be born before we reached our destination. Finally we arrived, I was placed on a medical table, and not long after Lidiya was born.

As I laid there the midwife starting asking me for my details, writing down the information. Your address she queried, "Troisdorf Camp" I answered. When she realised where I was from, all hell was let lose. "You swine" she screeched, "rouse, rouse"

I was made decent and the nurses helped me off the table (I see it like a big picture before my eyes). I was taken to the medical barrack, this was 12 March 1944. Imagine, maybe 15/20 minutes after giving birth, dressed in a thin cotton gown, knickers, coat and boots, I was led across the yard to this barrack. It was snowing and cold. I lay down, feeling ill and in agony, I started to cry.

Next day a visitor came, it was Andre a Frenchman, who lived and worked in the camp. A nice lad, who Misha had asked if he could bring me a letter. Andre managed to find me, and brought me some black bread (rye) and a letter from my husband. I still have got a copy of that letter that I was so comforted to receive in March 1944.

Letter from Dad (Michael to Mama (Katya) – 15 March 1944

Barracks Siegburg Near Cologne

Good day *(probably night)*

My darling Katinka, kissing you strongly, warmly. You and our little Lidochka. Katya I'm writing to you at the time of break, 12th hour. I gave the things you asked for to Paulina, but she didn't achieve anything at the hospital and brought it back. Now I keep thinking that maybe I can send it with Andre with whom I'm sending the supplies.

Beloved if only you knew how I worry about you especially your health. Maybe you need something, be good and convey through Andre. I've sent marks *(money)* for bread. If possible Andre will

change them for white bread and get it to you. I'm very much, very much asking you, don't get upset at the time of disturbance (air raid bombings). Look after yourself and our little crumb for who we both have to care for ourselves. Katinka darling, forgive me for writing so little, break is finishing *(break for dinner?)*

Well for the time being goodbye.

Kissing you and Lidochka, your husband and father.

(Right) Dad Misha with co-worker

The baby whom we named Lidiya, (Lidiya thinks she was named after a cousin of Misha), had difficulty feeding. They would start slapping her bottom, tapping her head trying to wake her to feed. I hadn't much milk in my breasts for her to suckle; she was in a poor state. Michael arrived, I picked up the baby and we returned to Troisdorf camp by trolley bus.

Arriving back at the camp the baby was taken away from me, she was placed in the camp kindergarten. The work I was sent to do was in the German canteen, to prepare vegetables for the German patrons, peeling onion, potatoes etc. This was five days after the birth. Then I was sent back to my old duties at the factory. The routine was for me to return to the nursery at dinner (lunch) time and evenings to breast feed her. In between she was fed by the nursery staff by bottle.

It was April; I recall the baby was maybe five or six weeks old. I looked through the window, all eleven babies

Barracks Troisdorf near Sigburg Mam with Lidiya

that were in the nursery were laying in their little cots outside. I don't know why they'd put them outside, perhaps they were experimenting. Going over to the nursery to see the baby I saw her (Lidiya) half naked, dressed only in a vest. Touching her she felt like a piece of ice. Grabbing her, shaking her I ran to the barrack that was the nursery screaming, "she's dead! She's dead!" wailing, showing the woman my baby. "Oh take her away" she snapped. "Take her to your barrack." Maybe she thought she'd died. From those 11 babies only 2 survived. The others were gassed. When Germany started losing the war, they gassed all those kids.

I ran to my barrack then went to the canteen to get some hot water. Pouring it into a bottle, I wrapped her in a blanket, placing the hot bottle near her. It appeared to be forever, she made no sign of life, sitting, my arms holding her, praying. She gave a gasp and opened her eyes. I blew into her mouth gently, relieved she was alive.

145

I kept her in the barrack. Our room had two families and now a baby. I was given an old pram by a German lady that lived near the camp and worked with me. The authorities allowed me a small amount of porridge and half a pint of milk a day for the baby.

My husband had repaired a watch for a German farmer. The farmer in gratitude started to bring me milk, as my breasts were not making much milk, this gift was appreciated. It became a regular thing, as he was delivering milk to the camp and to the cottages where the Germans lived, he passed our barrack. As I stood at the door he poured me milk into a container from his churn.

Once standing at the door of the barrack I glimpsed a uniform and realised he was following the farmer. As the farmer was walking towards me I said, "keep walking you're being watched." So the brave man devised another way of getting milk to me. He would leave the milk in some bushes, between the factory and the cottages, for me to pick up on my way back from work. Another thing he would do would be to give me coupons, saying if I was caught and he was questioned he would say he didn't know that we couldn't have his milk. The old farmer risked a lot with his kind actions.

The next experience I had with the baby was when she was taken ill. I asked for someone to see her, a Foyks Deutch Polish doctor came. He examined her, then he told me she would have to be taken to the medical barrack, as she had pneumonia. I'd had a little experience of nursing so my answer was, "No, I'll look after her, just leave what medicines you can, I'll nurse her." Putting compresses on her and doing what I could she eventually recovered, although later on, she again suffered with pneumonia.

Our life changed when Lidiya was born. I fed her with what milk I had in my breasts. When the police were not about, we would close the door, then bring out our electric ring that we had hidden under the bed, so we could cook something or warm things up. The pram was placed away from the wooden sides of the barrack, and I placed containers with water round the pram, so the bugs wouldn't bite her, but what the little black bugs did was to climb up the wall on to the ceiling, and drop down on her as she lay in the pram. The nappies were old rags I'd brought from the factory. To wash these "nappies" I had to use cold water, scrubbing with a stone to try and clean them. No fire, no hot water, we lived as best we could.

When I went to work at the factory friends looked after Lidiya until Michael returned from his shift. The kind German farmer continued to provide us with milk, and my nice German lady who had given me a pram, gave me bread or sugar and other bits of luxury she could spare. We got by.

Once I went to work with a big abscess on my hand. Arriving at the factory they sent me to the office for a medical man to see me. He looked at my hand, then they (the police) knocked me off my feet. Holding me down the doctor cut my abscess, it was packed with lint, then I was sent back to my work. I still have the scar to remind me.

The second time I got an abscess on my knee. The same procedure, held down while it was lanced. Pushing the pram with Lidiya in it I hobbled away. On my way back to the camp there was an air raid, I was passing the German cottages, so hid in one of the sheds.

Nineteen forty four, Christmas was a very bad time. Germany was losing the war, the camp police were getting more aggressive, their behaviour becoming nastier towards the camp workers.

One night the bombing raids began. Instead of hiding in the flimsy underground shelters we stayed in our barrack, we'd had enough, if we died we died. Eventually the raids ceased. Going outside we saw a few bombs had dropped in the camps, snapping some barbed wire fence. The camp police were nowhere to be seen, probably hiding in their bunkers. Taking the pram, putting Lidiya and what belongings we had in it, we covered the pram with a blanket taking the chance to get away from the camp.

There was smoke and fire everywhere as we made our way through the small town of Troisdorf. The place was lit up with bonfires, making night into day. Citizens of the town screaming, crying for help, some bodies strewn about. Quickly, quickly we made our way through that horrid street, as twenty minutes after the first raid the second wave started dropping bombs. We turned left going into the woods, as we watched, we saw our place being destroyed.

When my friends returned home after the war, one of them told my mum that I had been killed in a bombing raid in Cologne. My mum had a service for me in the church to my memory. When I wrote to her in 1958 she couldn't believe that I was still alive.

We came out of the woods and started walking, walking, walking. As I said it was around Christmas time. The snow lay thick on the ground, tree boughs with a covering of snow, making it look like a scene from a Christmas card. Passing a farm we asked for help, the farmer let us in. We told him we were Foyks Deutch (Germans) from Russia. Feeling pity for us he gave us a little food and some clothes for Lidiya. (Poor thing, she never cried, just lay there in the pram).

Sigh – We carried on walking, walking until we reached the main road where we joined other travellers heading to goodness knows where. Dusk was starting to fall. Because the Germans were losing battles countless numbers were evacuating, all heading away from the front line. As we trudged on, we had a feeling we were being followed, as every time I glanced round, I kept seeing the same man not far behind us. We started to get nervous, thinking maybe we'd got recognised as foreigners, and would be taken to the camps.

As we continued on our way he approached us saying in German, "Vas nationality are you?" "Why?" I asked. "I'm a Ukrainian", he answered. "O ya Ookrayinka" (I'm a Ukrainian) I replied. "Where are you going?" he queried. "I don't know, we're just walking, we don't know where" I said, telling him we were Foyks Deutch. He gave us some advice. "Don't go down this road, it's terrible, it's bad, camps, no cover, no food, bombings, people are dying like flies. If you take the path over that hill" he said, pointing at a narrow way, "on the other side, in the valley there is a small factory; there are some Foyks Deutch working there and a very good boss". After thanking him and saying goodbye we set off up the hill.

You see God/fate sent someone to us.

The path was covered in snow as we set off up the steep hill. Michael was angry, frustrated, as we struggled with our pram and belongings upwards. "You're stupid" he shouted. "Listening to people telling you where to go! Maybe the camps weren't that bad." We arrived on the top of the hill. Looking down and on to the other side, we saw a house on a hill amongst the trees, and in the valley a small factory with what appeared to be a barrack nearby. A river was semi-circling the factory.

As it was Christmas time everything was closed, the factory was not working, so we decided to head up to the house to talk to the boss. Nearing the house Michael said, "You go and ask if we can stay at the factory." Later I was to find out, before the war, he had a larger factory in a town, but when the war started he moved to this smaller one in the countryside, taking his mother, wife and children.

When we arrived, another couple were there talking to him. I started to ask him if he'd got room for us in his factory. I told him we were Foyks Deutch from Russia, (I always had to lie to survive) evacuees escaping from the bombings in Cologne. He said we could stay, saying to the other couple "You see you can find work easier, these people have a baby and don't stand much chance of anyone taking them in."

He appeared to be a kind man, giving us some food; he took us to the barrack. He gave us room in the barrack. Half was for Michael me and the baby and a girl whose name was Tanya. The other half was where the Foyks Deutch family from Odessa lived. The father, mother, three daughters and a young son, they worked at the factory. Providing us with a ration book he said, "You can help yourselves to what I have in the cellar, so you can cook your dinner." In the cellar potatoes, cabbage and carrots were stored, so we would not be hungry. It was a lace making factory and after the Christmas break we started work. Everything was working out, when we were at work the family from Odessa looked after Lidiya, when they were working I looked after their boy.

Life had become rather pleasant. Sundays were a free day, other workers would come from surrounding farms, we would chatter, sing for a while, feel light hearted. It was some distance from town, a long way away from the bombing raids. Although in the distance Germans were firing rockets and as they flew over our barracks then there was a deafening noise.

(I have forgotten a lot of incidents but I'm trying to remember).

To reach the factory you had to go over a bridge. The boss told us to build a tunnel shelter near the factory, in case the bridge was destroyed, so we had somewhere to hide. Everyone was retreating, as the front was advancing towards us.

Mama giggles as she recalls this.

One night there was a knock on the door. Opening the door we saw four Russian POWs still in uniform, they were escapees. We told them to come in. After introductions Tanya and I told them to undress, leading them to a small corridor we covered them over with blankets, then closed the door so they could not be seen. We then spent the night washing their underwear, sending word to the farm workers for civilian clothes. The next day the Russians put on the civvies and continued on their way. We later disposed of their Russian uniforms. A similar incident happened with three Italian POWs whom we hid in our barrack.

The road nearby often had people passing by, civilians, soldiers, prisoners. Tanya and I would go and take a bucket of potatoes or carrots and hand them out to prisoners as they were marched by. One day the boss came to query why we were using so many potatoes. "I don't know why the stocks are going down! " I said. He replied "you see you must be careful, the war, the front advancing there may not be the chance to get anymore food." So that was it, we stopped giving out "our" potatoes.

One day we saw American tanks passing down the road and soldiers heading up the hill. We were hiding behind our shelter, the next thing there was a commotion at the back of us. There were maybe a dozen German soldiers and their officer, they were shouting and fighting. The officer was ordering them to march forward; the soldiers were refusing, throwing away their rifles, taking off their German uniform jackets and tossing them on the ground.

Then we saw an American tank heading for our bridge with guns pointing our way. If they had decided to shoot, we would all have been blown to bits. As the German officer continued screaming orders, the soldiers, his men, ignored him, the officer retreated. It's an awful feeling, seeing men arms held above their heads, trembling with fear.

The tank stopped, then the Americans brought down the boss and all his family into the factory yard where we were stood. "How have you been treated?" the Americans asked. "Was he cruel?" We answered, all agreeing. "He was a very good boss and had treated us as human beings." In this way we protected him, if we said he had been bad they would have shot him, no arguments.

Chapter Twenty One

END OF THE WAR

The front arrived. The Americans had liberated us; everyone was so happy, joyous, that we at last were free. The Foyks Deutch from Russia continued to work for the lace factory after the war. We carried on living, we managed to get food, as we had the ration books given to us by our boss, and of course the vegetables he allowed us to have. On a few occasions, marauders tried to get across the bridge, to attack our boss and his family. All of us including the Foyks Deutch from Russia always tried to protect them.

Everywhere people started celebrating, drinking, rejoicing that the war was over, but after the front had left, how things turned terribly to cruelty. Lots of arms were being discarded; Michael carried a pistol he had found. It was as if hell had been let loose. Hundreds of refugees, released prisoners, forced labour workers, who were now free to go where they pleased, were on the move through the valley.

Screaming could be heard from various areas as the displaced wandered through. Some were getting drunk going berserk, raping women and children. It was horrific! Attacking German farmers, workers, people who had done no harm to anyone, just trying to survive, but revenge was being taken on the innocent as well as the guilty.

When I worked at the factory there was a foreman who was in charge. No matter what we did he didn't report us. Sometimes we'd go to the toilet and drop to sleep leaving our machines not working. He would just come into the toilets and wake us to go back to work; he never ever hit us or reported us. He was a good man, a father of five children. One day he went to the woods to collect wood for his fire. A group of men approached him; I don't know what nationality, Russian or Polish? They wanted his watch, when he refused they killed him.

Different nationalities were now trying to make their way home. I said to my husband, "Right I'm heading home, I want to go home." My husband went to the Soviet camp. "My wife is a Ukrainian and wants to go home." They told him I had to go to the Russian camp. On his return, he told me the procedure for my return to my homeland. "But" he added "If you want to go, you go, but you are not taking Lidiya with you!" This argument ended in a fight. You can see my finger where it didn't set properly after being broken in this dispute.

Rumours of treatment of the Soviet people who were returning started to be heard. The Soviets – Stalin – thought of the forced labour workers as enemies of the state, traitors to the motherland even though the majority had no choice. Treatment in the Soviet DP camps was strict and the discipline severe.

If a girl arrived at the camp with a baby and no husband her hair was shorn off. On their return to the motherland, their beloved motherland, many of the repatriates were sent to Siberia etc to serve time in camps as traitors. If they had children the children were taken into government care.

One day Michael came into the barrack, he had been drinking. "Is there something to eat?" he asked. He was wearing pilot boots, the large leather fur lined ones." "No" I answered, "I didn't know when you'd be back." He kicked me. Maybe that's why I have a hernia. The Germans beat me in the stomach for striking, my husband would hit me in the stomach or head when he was drunk. Since being a small child there has always been someone to beat me.

1980 – 5 years ago when we were talking about the incident he said he had thrown them.

I survived, I'm a survivor. I want to write everything as I remember it, so my children can know my life. If they're interested?

Our next place of residence was a Polish DP camp Kolnehiem; previously I think it had been a German soldier's administrative place. The Germans were evicted out of their living quarters and the rooms were given to DP people. The reason we were allowed in the Polish camp, was that although Michael's mother was a Ukrainian, his father was Polish. We were given a "flat" (rooms) and Michael was given a job servicing and repairing electrics, telephones etc.

The camp was being visited by English or American personnel, enquiring about Soviet or Ukrainian nationals, as they were being repatriated back to their homes, even if it was against their will. The next evening the Russians were arriving to take "their" people home, but as was later known, the "homes" that they were deported to were prison camps or Siberia, for on average a five year sentence. The crime committed was treason, traitor to the motherland for working for the enemy, even though there was no choice. I recently discovered a friend of mine who had returned had served a five year sentence.

Christmas 1945/46 It was so nice; I had managed to get a Christmas tree. I had Lidiya, after all the turbulence that I'd gone through I felt at peace. New Year was approaching and the Polish officers were organising a party to celebrate the beginning of what was hopefully to be a new peaceful start to the coming year.

Michael, who had taken umbrage at not being invited, was really miffed. At about five minutes to midnight, as everyone was getting jolly, exuberant, waiting for twelve o'clock, the camp was plunged into darkness. It was Michael! He had been drinking of course, so to get his revenge at not being invited to the festivities, he made sure to spoil the officers get together by switching the electricity off at the mains.

Next thing there was a knocking on my door, it was the camp police. "Where's your husband?" they asked. "I don't know" I replied. "He's in for it when we find him. Someone's switched the lights off, we're sure it's him, we want to find him!" they said as they left. Later when he returned I asked him "Misha it was you wasn't it. Why?" "Oh let them learn to enjoy partying in the dark" was the answer.

Life carried on, nothing much happened. Then there was an incident. We had friends in the camp, one being an engineer, someone important, a large built man who had run away, escaped from the Soviets during, or after the war? My husband and the engineer were walking along outside the camp. As they strolled along, a car stopped, a door opened and our friend was bundled in the back and driven away. After that event, my husband was very frightened to go outside the camp. Incidents like that used to happened.

In Cologne outside the camp was a building that housed some West Ukrainian girls. Raids were carried out by Soviet authorities; they had the right to take the girls back to their homeland. When they saw the Soviets coming they would run and hide, sometimes behind our camp gates which were guarded by Polish and English soldiers.

Once I was looking through the window in my barrack, and a raid was being made by the Russian soldiers, who were taking the West Ukrainian girls against their will to a lorry, that was standing by. The Polish soldiers stood and observed what was happening and as the Russian soldiers went to collect more girls, the Polish soldiers opened the doors of the lorry, releasing them and letting them into our camp, where the Russians had no jurisdiction.

Making friends with a lovely, calm warm family led me down another path in my life. Their name was Volhovchik, they were Baptists. I was introduced by them to the bible, which I had never read and I started to study the good book, becoming a believer in Cologne in 1946. About this time I became pregnant with my second baby Val, or Valentina as she was christened. I continued studying the bible and going to Baptist church. My strengthening belief in a God brought me peace, and I prayed to him, thanking him for being alive and surviving the war.

My husband on the other hand turned to partying, gathering lots of friends, having found comfort in alcohol. After his friends left he would be nasty, sometimes violent. As time went on Michael turned more to drink and I to religion.

The next lap of our journey. From the Polish camp we were sent to Kavener? Near the Belgian border. At this place was a hospital, most of it had been turned into premises for refugees. It had been a psychiatric hospital and part of it still housed "mental patients" as they were called then. Here at Kaven?Kavelar? I went into labour with Valya. I was taken to the main building, where I was helped up the steps by a nun. To this day, I remember the nun being very masculine and couldn't help but think the nun was a man. The nun took me to the bathroom, petting my stomach. I don't know why, but I was scared. So, near the Belgium border my Valichka (Val) was born.

Lindorf camp was our next port of call. Here in Lindorf there were quite a few Baptists, so I was amongst friends. It was at this time in 1947, when my husband, with other male refugees, sailed to England to find work and a place to stay. This they had to do, before they could send for their wives and families.

Polish DP Camp Dusseldorf Germany. Mum on the right Lidiya on the right in the pram, sister Valya on the left.

Here in Lindorf my Valichka was taken ill, she was in such a bad way that she was taken to hospital, where I stayed by her side. Thank God she recovered.

I continued trying to live by the Evangelist way of life. Orthodox religion had no interest for me. All the pomp and ceremony, which in my eyes, made little difference to peoples way of life, the drinking the squabbling etc. The Baptists way of living, their lives appealed to me more, from what I was reading in the bible. The respect the family showed each other, the consideration of the husband and wife to each other. They did not smoke and drank only in moderation. Families helped and supported each other, so I was drawn to this way of life. Michael was weak and the path he was going on was destroying him. After a difficult episode with him I prayed and hoped God would change him.

As I said previously, I didn't want to go to England to join my husband, so writing to him, I explained my feelings. "You are now in England in a new place, I think now is the time we should go our separate ways." I had put down my name to go to Venezuela, as they were taking women with children. Michael wrote back promising he would change, that he would stop drinking, stop beating me. We would start a new life, begging me to go to him to bring his children. I weakened and decided to join him. At least my children will have their father; I consoled myself, remembering my animosity towards my stepfather. Lidochka and Valya will know how much their own father loved them, which he did.

Some women had already gone to their husbands in England. One wrote to her friend who was still at the camp. "I don't know what Katya is going to do, Michael is drinking a lot. I know he was a weak character, and could not come to terms with the events of the war, but I wrote "I'm not coming to you! You haven't changed." His answer "if you don't bring the children, I'll find you and knife you" he threatened. My answer "You can't you are too far away".

We began arguing by post. Then again the pleading, "please bring the children, I won't harm you, we can get divorced, but it will be better for the children here, there's everything here, better for them than living in a camp."

Meanwhile in England, Michael had lodgings with a family named Philips. Mrs Philips was a slight pretty woman whose husband was very ill, they had two children. When she heard I was coming to join my husband she was upset. "Why are you sending for them?" she asked Michael. "My husband will be dead soon, we could be together."

A neighbour, Mr Wordsworth had somehow found out about this, and told a friend of ours Stefka to let Michael know he had lodgings for him, his wife and children. Michael left Mrs Philips's house and went to Mr Wordsworth's home, where he was given two rooms, a bedroom and sitting room. Everything was now set, we would be lodging at "Grandad's" as we all called Mr Wordsworth and whenever spoken of to this day in our family he is known as Grandad, a good kind man.

Chapter Twenty Two

ARRIVAL IN ENGLAND

I started preparing for my journey to my husband in England. I was taking a cot with me that I had got in 1946 from a German lady who lived opposite the Polish DP camp in Cologne? The lady was maybe twenty eight years of age. She had slept in it as a child; also her two children had been raised in the same cot. The cot continued to be of good use for many a year, as I used it for all my six children, then my eldest daughter Lidiya's three children also had use of it.

The cot now is in a museum in Barnsley.

Starting the journey was not easy. Two small children, Lida, four years of age and Valya two, trailing from camp to camp with our possessions, first Munster then Copenhagen. We were travelling with some Christians (Baptists). Everyone helped each other, all friendly, all on the same destination. Wives going to their husbands, taking their children to meet their fathers, who they hadn't seen in a long time.

Crossing the sea we arrived in Harwich, where we were met by the Red Cross workers who were to help us on our journey. I remember going down the railway station platforms dragging Lidiya along, carrying Valya from one train to another. The carriages were always full, trailing from one carriage to another, but we never managed to get a seat. Eventually we ended up in the same carriage as Schutka, whose husband worked at the same place as Misha. Their place of work was a coal mine, Hickleton Main, where my husband was employed as an electrician. On the journey north we had to stand all the way.

I had written to Michael, asking him to find out if there were any Baptist churches near where he lived. He found a Baptist community, who held their meetings in a hall, in the mining village of Goldthorpe, adjoining Highgate where Misha lived, actually very close by. He introduced himself and told them about me.

Hickleton Main pit where Michael worked

Finally we arrived; I don't know what town or place it was. Michael was there waiting for us. Lidiya, as soon as she saw her Tato (Daddy in Polish/Ukrainian) went running towards him shouting, "Tato, Tato" but Valya, when Michael tried to take her to cuddle her, put her head on my shoulder, started crying and her arms wouldn't let go of my neck. Of course poor child she didn't know who he was. Misha's face was shining, happy, he was overjoyed that at last we were here with him and OK.

At his side were a couple, he introduced me to them, their names were Vera and Les Shepard. They were husband and wife from the Baptist church. They had a car, so offered to bring my husband to meet us and take us back to my new home. Les and Vera were such wonderful, kind people who were to introduce me to the other members of the Evangelical church, who were to support me spiritually in the years to come.

Baptist congregation Goldthorpe.
Bottom second right Katya, Vee by her side. Val 4th left, Lidiya 6th

At last I'd arrived at my destination, the house of Mr Wordsworth and his dog Spot, 34 William Street, Highgate, Goldthorpe, South Yorkshire. A mining village, the house where a new episode of my life was to begin.

On our arrival my friend Stefka Rysack came round to the house to greet us. Her husband's name was Ivan and Stefka

Grandad Wordsworth with his dog Spot outside his house at Highgate.

was pregnant with their first child a daughter they named Katrunya/ Katherine. They had lodgings close by. Schutka, the lady with whom I'd travelled with, also lived two houses down the street from me, with her daughter and husband who had managed to rent a couple of rooms there.

Grandad was very, very good to me and my family, kind and patient. All the same it was difficult, not understanding the English language, and when I had to start cooking on a "black lead fireplace" – Yorkshire Range, I really found it hard, trying to cook on an open fire, as at home we had stoves, a little similar to Aga cookers.

A couple of days after my arrival I was in "our" room when a young woman dashed in, followed by Grandad (maybe Mrs Philips?) She was asking for Mishka, I couldn't understand what else she was saying, but Grandad had raised his voice, shaking his finger at her saying, "Bad woman! Bad woman!" Maybe Michael had had a fling with her, I don't know, men are men, and when he'd had a drink who knows. He was handsome, so it would not be difficult for a lady to fall for him.

Michael had been in England a year when I arrived. Although he'd worked all that time, he had no money. Goodness knows what he'd spent it on, but never mind, I was a Christian, I forgave him and prayed to God to help him to change. He stopped drinking, maybe he would sneak a drink, I don't know, but, he was good to me.

I went to church, he didn't interfere, although he wasn't interested in going himself. I went to work at a farm, while grandad looked after Lidiya and Valya. Also I wrote to Baptists in Canada, they sent me some aid. Michael continued working at Hickleton Main colliery, we started saving money. At last we had hope of a future; Vyera was born in Highgate so now we had three beautiful daughters.

I will recall some amusing moments of being a foreigner and not understanding the language.

Walking from Highgate to Goldthorpe, there was a small shop standing just before the railway bridge, it was a grocery shop. As I passed by on my way home from, I forget where I'd been; I noticed these large oranges, so I went inside and bought some. Not waiting until I arrived home, I started peeling one, then eagerly putting a piece in my mouth. It was horrible, I spat it out. I peeled another one, then another one, all the oranges I tried were the same, bitter and sour, so I threw them all away into someone's garden. I was so upset. When I got home Michael was there, bursting into tears I cried, "These English! Because I'm a foreigner they've sold me bad oranges." Later I was to find out the oranges were actually grapefruits!

Another incident was when I needed an onion, going next door to borrow one. That's how things were in those days. Looking into my dictionary for a translation of the word onion, (Tiboolya – onion) underneath (Terkva – church). So looking the word onion up, accidentally I read the word beneath (Tiboolya – church). Off I went next door to my neighbours, with the word church for onion. You can imagine the conversation. "You have church?" "Yes we go to church." "Me have church?" "Yes you go to church." Seeing some onions near the sink, I pointed at them, but couldn't get them to understand. Again I went home in tears. "They wouldn't give me an onion, they pretended they didn't know what I was saying." Now it's amusing, but it wasn't then.

Lidiya started school by following the other children. One morning I was looking for her. Just as I started to worry a lady brought her home holding her hand she said, "Is this your little girl?" "Yes" I replied. "We found her in the school" she said. Unbeknown to me she had put on her coat and followed the neighbour's children to school.

Another incident is very difficult to write about.

I remember the incident even though I was only four or five – Lidiya

In Highgate, near a dog racing track, a small stream runs through the fields. This is where a young man took a few girls, Lidiya being amongst them, to show some boys how sex was performed. When I noticed my little girl was missing, I panicked and ran searching for her. I found them by the stream, with the man on top of one of the girls, who was aged eleven, maybe twelve. The other children were playing in the stream. Jumping across the stream, I grabbed hold of the "boy", he was sixteen or seventeen, and I started screaming and dragging him onto the ground, beating him.

Neighbours, who had all been helping in the search, came running and pulled me off him. The police came and talked to the children. Apparently, he'd sent the little ones away to play, while he raped the girl, showing a twelve year old by what a boy does to a girl. Not long after, the family moved away. Yes it was horrible not something I choose to remember.

Life was pleasant. I had a lot of friends, I went to meetings at the Baptist church, and Christians would visit me. Also Michael was working in the coalmine, and gradually we had enough money saved for a deposit for a house with the help I received from writing to Baptists in Canada, who also sent us donations.

Darfield, a couple of miles away, was where we bought our first house, 24 Church View, on 22 May 1950. It was in a lovely spot. The previous owners were Mr and Mrs Holmes who had one daughter, Anne. The Holmes family moved to Scarborough.

Katya, our mama and Mrs Holmes kept contact and were friends for the rest of their lives.

It was a terraced house, and at the top of the street there was a stone wall. Behind the wall, if you looked over, ran the river Dearne and across the other side, a playing field with an old stone pub, the Bridge Inn, at the other side. Our house was the third house down from the river, two rooms downstairs, and three bedrooms upstairs. The kitchen door opened straight onto the street, where across the unpaved street was an outbuilding. At the front of the outbuilding was a small covered area, where metal dustbins were kept. If you went to the back of the brick outbuildings you would find two separate toilets, one to share between two families.

The back of the terraced houses all had separate gardens, with fields at the back of them, the river meandering by. Then across the river, a hill with the wonderful sight of Darfield Parish church on the top, though through the trees, only the tower of the nine hundred year old church could be seen, rising above.

We furnished the house with second hand furniture that we managed to acquire. In the kitchen, along one side of the room, we had a black horsehair chaise lounge, when the children sat on it, they always moaned, as it prickled their bottoms. In the centre of the kitchen a large wooden table that was used for everything. Eating meals, baking, preparing meals, and ironing. It was the only table – come – worktop in the house. Of course the traditional Yorkshire range for heat, cooking, baking and boiling water. In the bedrooms were two iron beds with flock, lumpy mattresses, and my beloved cot that I had brought from the DP camp. In the garden I planned to grow flowers, vegetables and keep chickens. Later, a good neighbour, Mr Paradine helped me get an allotment. Life was good.

On a Sunday I would take the children with little Vyera in a pushchair and walk the two or three miles to Goldthorpe where the Baptist hall was. I received help from a charity in America. This was of great help, food, second hand clothes; also I made my children's clothes.

Katya and Misha after liberation in happier times

Michael loved to read, draw, sing and play the guitar. He didn't really suit digging, but he helped in other ways. We were happy.

After years of trauma and uncertainty, not knowing whether we would live or die, this England felt safe, peaceful and we could try and live without fear.

EPILOGUE

We were the only foreign family in Darfield, although there was a Russian man, Fyeda who married an English woman, who already had 2 or 3 children, and a Ukrainian bachelor, Karpo who lived at the other side of the village.

Our mama Katya Alexandrovna was a strong woman, though the trauma of war, death, partings were behind her she still had more heartache to face, strange land, unknown customs, people whose language she did not yet understand. Not knowing whether her beloved family in the Ukraine were alive or dead. Not daring to write home in case the NKVD (Secret Police) would find them and take them back. So she continues to tell us the other phase of her life.

Vyera had been born in Highgate, Goldthorpe on 14th April 1950. She was a beautiful baby, blonde curly hair, big eyes. I had three children and didn't want anymore. Then it happened, pregnant, I was so upset. I was a couple of weeks late and started to panic, putting my feet into hot water, trying other old wives remedies. Nothing worked and later in the pregnancy it was too late.

Well 2nd March 1952 my twins were born. Anna was born first, such a plump little thing, then Michael, so skinny, like a skeleton. I had been in hospital for 6 weeks; meanwhile a home help came daily to help Michael look after the 3 children left at home. On my return with the babies, I had a surprise that I wasn't happy about; Michael had spent the money I had saved for a pram on a car.

Mr H Tasker, a good man and friend had helped him; the problem was Michael started driving on a provisional licence. If I said anything to him, suggesting he may get into trouble, he'd answer "I'm a mechanic, an engineer!" He didn't believe he had to pass a driving test. Never mind, everything was good, we were happy.

When he first arrived in England he was employed as an electrician. As time went on he started to experience nasty tricks played on him at work. At first he tried to ignore what was happening, thinking it would eventually stop. One of the "jokes" was he'd get a report that there was a problem at the coal face, it was a long way to walk and when he arrived and checked, no problem had been reported and there was nothing wrong.

Walking back to the pit bottom, he would have stones thrown at him. Though he suspected who could be behind this, (A twins) he was never sure. Michael started being on edge, he got so unnerved it got to the stage where he was afraid to go to work.

The other fear we both had was the dread of the NKVD (the Russian Secret Police). We had entered the Polish DP camps as West Ukrainian, although we were actually from the East Ukraine which had been under Soviet rule. We were cautious what we said and to whom because if the Russians had placed spies amongst us and our deception was disclosed we would be forced back to the Soviet Union.

Those fears may have been unfounded, but rumours were abound in the Ukrainian community that Ukrainian people had gone missing in Wolverhampton, Oldham, Bradford. Tales were spread of doors being answered in the early hours of the morning and individuals vanishing, kidnapped. So that pressure was always with us.

Stalin died in 1953, yet it took me another 5 years to pluck up the courage to write back home to Torez to let my family know I was alive, this was 1958. I didn't know if anyone was still left alive to answer my letter. Fortunately I eventually got to know that my mama, sister and brothers had all survived those terrible times. I corresponded with my mama and sister but it was 1970s? before I dare go back to the Donbas.

Mum paid £100 to the authorities for permission to go to her village/town Torez from Donetsk. She was loaned a car and driver. In those days the only way to go on holiday to the Soviet Union was by organised Intourist groups. It was frowned on to go off the planned route. Torez is maybe 20 miles from Donetsk, half an hour by car.

Taking my granddaughter Tracey I returned both excited and scared. After all these years I was reunited with my sister, brothers, and relatives visiting the small cottage where I had last seen my mother in the 1940s. The heartache I felt as I knelt at her grave, tears falling on the mound for the years that had been lost.

Now I'll return to my story. From 1945 I handled my stress by praying, often getting on my knees to ask God for strength. Michael handled his fear by anaesthetising his anxiety with alcohol. I still cannot stand the smell of gin, which was his preferred drink.

Michael continued driving his car with no learner plates, no qualified driver with him and only a provisional licence. Well I think someone used to report him, I know it's a sin to accuse but my suspicions fell on a Mr Bun.

Anyway, one day he drove down Church View turned left heading for Doncaster Road, which was a short distance away. He'd just got on to the main road and the police stopped him. Michael was fined and banned from driving for 6 months. The ban did not deter him, he risked driving again, and he got fined again. Never mind he was good to me, gentle. We worked hard and I could say from 1948 to 1952 we were happy. I with the children would travel to Baptist meetings to Bradford, Manchester, Huddersfield; my faith gave me some kind of strength.

This particular day Michael came home, coming through the door I could see he was upset and shook up. "What's wrong?" I asked. He started to try and explain that he had been in an accident. The accident had happened at Darfield crossroads, where Camplejohns garage stood. A delivery lorry had run into his car, luck was on his side as the car had overturned many times, but Michael had escaped with just a few bruises and a bang to his head.

Mr Cooper the driver of the lorry appealed to Michael's weak nature, asking him not to report the incident, it would influence his employer and he could lose his job. My husband admitted to Mr Cooper that he only had a provisional driving licence, so it was agreed that Michael would not report the accident to the police and Mr Cooper would pay for the repair of the car. I told him "just wait and see, he will report the crash to the police and you will be at fault."

From the back of our house looking towards the church, across the river, a path could be seen, descending down the path I saw 2 policemen heading our way, obviously coming from the police station that was on Church Street. "See Mishka!" I shouted "I told you, if you'd had reported it you would just have got a fine for having no L plates!" The police questioned him, looked at the damage to the car. Again he was fined.

During this time, 1954, his problems began, or may I say became more noticeable. Misha started drinking more than usual, reluctant to go to work, sometimes hiding. Neighbours used to express their opinions. "So and so Ciesliks – bloody foreigners" as he left one job then another. I was tired, overworked; tension began to build between us.

Again, he wanted to drive his car and decided this time he would go by the book. He asked Mr Tasker a friend who had a full licence to accompany him. As they headed along Doncaster Road towards Goldthorpe, he must have been speeding and someone took his registration. I don't know what happened next, but he let Mr Tasker out of the car, to make his way home across the fields. Michael didn't want Mr Tasker's kindness repaid by Mr Tasker getting into bother. This was the fourth time he'd ignored the law. The consequence was not just a fine.

The stress and fear of what would happen to him and his illness really took control of him. He tried to commit suicide by drinking methylated spirits and sleeping tablets. When the police came he was unsteady on his feet and collapsed. Don't forget in the 1950s it was a crime, illegal to try and take your own life. (Suicide was decriminalised in 1961). Misha was taken into custody to Armley jail in Leeds where he was put under medical observation for a week. The result was because of his war experience he'd suffered from a persecution complex.

(There are newspaper cuttings of the court case. Here are a few snippets).

Speaking in rapid broken English a woman made a long and tearful appeal to Barnsley West Riding Magistrates today to let her husband go home ....

He imagined he was being shadowed by various people such as British Secret Service .....

Cieslik asked to be allowed to go home to look after his wife and children but was told he would get a better chance to recover in hospital .....

Michael was just 34 years of age when he was placed in Storthes Hall Hospital Kirkburton.

Michael had left his latest job so, now on my own with 5 children. I applied for Social Security. By growing vegetables in the garden, keeping chickens, renting an allotment, also sewing my children's clothes I supplemented the money I received from the welfare. I tried the best I could.

A bus run by Camplejohns made a regular journey to Storthes Hall, taking relatives to visit their loved ones. I would visit him all the time, sometimes taking the children with me. Michael started to beg me to sign him out every time I visited him. The doctors advised against me signing him out of hospital saying, "Mr Cieslik is an ill man and needs treatment." All the same I signed him out, I felt so sorry for him. We'd had our problems in the past but he wasn't a bad man, just weak. I believed in God and had faith that he would help him.

I brought him home. The first 6 months he was signed on sick benefit, everything was Okay. Meanwhile I got pregnant with my sixth child, my youngest David. No feet in hot water here. I was desperate and for a split second the railway lines beckoned.

It was about this time he started to sink into depression. Nights, he did not go to bed, he'd go walk about. Sometimes getting lost. Once the police brought him home, saying he'd been found in Wakefield, wanting to drive home in someone's car. I now was 7 months pregnant. Michael started to act strange. He'd burst out laughing, would say that I looked ugly with my big belly. He used to love to hear me sing. On one occasion he insisted I had to sing for him. I sat there with my pregnant tummy and I started to sing but he kept interrupting saying, "Sing higher."

Oh such troubles began. Don't forget he was an ill man. He wouldn't go to the doctors to renew his sick note. Then to cap it all he gave his notice in at work. I tried living on the small amount of money I had saved. Trying to manage on that and what I grew. I also make crepe paper roses to sell. Life had become so difficult, the worst in England were the years 1954-55. Of course things were becoming tense between us. Arguing over what little money we had. Him needing his drink and cigs, I needed bread to feed us with.

I would find kitchen knives hidden under the mattress. It had got to the stage where I dare not get undressed for bed, going to bed and rising in the same clothes. Early morning rising to light the fire. Don't forget there was no gas or electric cooker; the fire had to be lit before even a kettle could be boiled. Although I did have a primus stove to use when I could afford the methylated spirits to fuel it.

One night he lost his mind all together, he started ranting and raving, waving a knife about. I got so frightened, maybe Lidiya remembers. I went upstairs and woke her saying, "Lida! Valya! Help me!" I picked Vyera up in my arms and they got the twins, Michael and Ann. We went into the small bedroom that had a single bed, a small electric fire. Also the door had a lock that worked, the locks on the 2 larger bedrooms were broken. Michael rarely went to bed at night. This small bedroom was where I used to go to have a lie down.

I tell you it just took minutes for me, Lidiya and Val to get all the children into that small room and lock the door. A little later, still shouting he started banging on the door. "My Dad's in the other room being murdered by the NKVD." His Father had been an officer in the Austro-Hungarian army. Abuse started to be hurdled at me as he yelled "you …… bitch doing nothing to try and save him, nothing to help him." "Misha, Misha" I begged. "Your Dad isn't here." I started pleading with him. "They're beating my Father! They're beating my Father!" He was knocking and banging on the door. This continued for I don't know how long. Then he went quiet.

An idea had come to me. If I tied strips of bed sheets together and tied Lidiya on to end, then lowered her down, Lidiya could go to Mrs Robinson who was a neighbour, a good woman and she would help us. I never gave a thought of knocking on the wall to the next door or shouting. I didn't want anyone to know the "bloody foreigners" shame. So I started ripping a sheet using my teeth to start the tear. Everything was quiet on the other side of the door. Early hours of the next day, after what appeared to be a long time that there had been silence, I decided to open the door.

Telling Lidiya to keep the children in the room I put an eiderdown in front of me and quietly opened the door. The reason for placing the eiderdown in front of me was that if he went for me I could throw the eiderdown over him, knock his legs from under him and keep him there until the children escaped.

I went into the other bedroom, Michael was laid on the bed fast asleep, I covered him with the eiderdown, whispering to Lidiya, "Take the children downstairs, very quietly." Lida took the children downstairs, I followed. The stairs led straight into the kitchen. At the bottom of the stairs was a door which had a lock on it. I locked it and went to fetch Dr Wileszinski.

Life had become very bad. Fear, fear for maybe a month before he was taken back. When the ambulance came to take him he said to me "What kind of wife have I got, the NKVD are taking me and she's just sat watching." This was March 17th 1955. Michael was in a long time (maybe 5 or 6 years?). I would visit him regularly, as I said sometimes taking the children with me to see their Dad.

Maybe a couple of days after Michael had been taken back to Storthes Hall, I had a visit from the Social Services. It was a Mrs Thompson, she lived in Darfield. "You're pregnant" she stated. "Have you anyone to look after your children and you?" she enquired. I was washing clothes on a rubbing board. A mangle stood nearby with a pile of clothes on the floor ready for washing (no washer). The kiddies were sitting on the settee. (This was a horsehair stuffed chaise lounge). They had been bathed and were dressed in clean clothes.

To her question of who would look after us I answered, "I will look after me and my children." "We thought we would take the children for a short time, while you get on your feet" she continued. "Oh no! no!" I replied. She looked at the children, then went to look at the rooms upstairs. Coming downstairs she again tried talking me into letting the children go to foster parents. My answer was, "They're going nowhere unless it's over my dead body!" She went away coming back a couple of days later to formalise things. I felt as if a stone had been lifted from my heart. No more fear, no more worrying of where he was, or what he was up to. My youngest child was born on 23rd April 1955. I named him David Alexander.

After the Social Welfare's visit I started to receive Social Security money. With the help of the Baptists I received food parcels and second hand clothes from America and UNRA (United Nations Relief Admin). I also had postal foster parents for the twins, Michael's was in Canada a Mr Wilson and Ann's was in America. From these foster parents we also received parcels and sometimes money. With this additional help I started to have a decent living.

Meanwhile everytime I visited Michael he appeared to be getting worse. He wanted to run away and accused them of beating him. I don't know how much truth there was in that but I do know he had two gold teeth pulled out. On some of my visits he would look at me with hate filled eyes demanding I bring him whiskey and cigarettes. "Misha" I said. "They're trying to make you better."

Well he didn't get better. The doctors wanted to do an operation of his head (brain?). "Is it guaranteed to cure him?" I asked, the answer was "No only fifty-fifty chance." "If you think it will make him well then do the operation. But I'm not signing anything, I'm not having it on my conscious if anything goes wrong" I replied. He didn't have an operation, but he did have electric shock treatment.

I continued visiting Michael up to the early sixties. A year before he was released he stayed in the hospital and was allowed to go out to work on a daily basis *(I think our Dad worked doing odd jobs at a cotton mill nearby – Lid).*

The time for his release approached. Memories flooded back of the weeks before he was taken to hospital. The fear I'd lived through the hard work, him not going to work, his drinking or just laying in bed talking rubbish. It had been hell.

The advice I was given from a doctor at the hospital was, "Mrs Cieslik let him go his own way. You look after your children because when he is released and comes across alcohol he will drink, he's been damaged by the war. He won't change." What choice did I have? I followed the doctor's advice, I had six children relying on me, their mother, they had no one else. I went to the solicitors and the courts gave me a legal separation.

Dad – Although separated, when in years to come our Mam got to know our Dad had a flat in Salford she did all she could to make his life a little better. When he died after a heart attack our Mam made all the arrangements for him to be brought back home to Darfield where he was buried in Darfield church yard.

In August, Victor Harasymchuk a West Ukraine bachelor came to lodge with me. Victor needed a room, I needed coal. You see he was a coal miner and received a free coal allowance as part of his wages. Also the lodging money was useful of course. It was a solution to both our problems a great help for me.

Uncle Victor as we called him never married and had no family, only a distant cousin in West Ukraine. He stayed with our family many years. After he had passed away our Mother made sure he had a decent funeral. His ashes were taken to the Ukraine by Lidiya, who passed them to his cousin, who arranged for the ashes to be scatter on Victor's Mam's grave.

The council gave us a new house on an estate that was being built at the bottom of Church View. I felt so lucky, it had an inside toilet and a bathroom. These homes felt like palaces and were built in the cornfield where the children had played when they were small.

I don't know what else to say. Lida, Valya, you most of all suffered. I can remember how you used to help me make paper roses till your small fingers were blistered. Can you remember how we sat in front of our fireplace (Yorkshire Range) pegging rugs. Of course you do! I thank God for all my children and love you all.

The years went by then I met Ernest (Brummit) who cared and looked after me, loved me. As you know he's helped me all he could. Without his help I could not have helped my children or sent all those parcels to my relatives in the Ukraine for the last seven years. *(Ernest was there for her for the rest of her life – Lid).* I could have married Ernest, but I've been my own boss for too long. As it is said "Your home, your truth."

I love my home at least in my old age I can look through my living room window, see the view on the hill of old Darfield church, see the tall tree near to where my husband's grave is.

Mama Katya's beloved view from her window

Dear children there's nothing much to say, I've already talked a lot.

What I want for you all, when my days are done, and I've gone away, is that you look after one another. It is said you can't choose your relatives, only your friends. Love one another. I know it's difficult. It's difficult for me now I'm older. When some of mine talk to me, as if I'm an old woman they think I'm a silly old woman…..but never mind!

*Mama and her sister Valya and brothers
Vitya, Mitya and Sasha*

*Mama and her sister and brothers on her first visit home
Sasha, Mama, Valya, Mitya, Vitya knelt down*

EKATERINA ALEXANDROVA stood at the roots in the birth and development of friendly ties between the twinned towns of Gorlovka and Barnsley (Great Britain).

Up to the Second World War EKATERINA TECLIK lived near the town of Gorlovka and was elected a member of the Gorcom Comsumol.

In 1941 she left at the occupation by the fascists of our territories. EKATERINA ALEXANDROVA was taken away by the fascists to Germany. She was freed by American soldiers in 1945.

For political reasons EKATERINA ALEXANDROVA TECLIK did not return to the CCCP after the war and went to live permanently in England, namely in the village of Darfield near Barnsley. She was active in keeping contact with Gorlovka. When those ties were established she was one of the first to welcome our delegation in England. All following delegations invariably met EKATERINA ALEXANDROVA.

Every member of the delegations especially the children invariably felt the great love and attention of EKATERINA ALEXANDROVA.

On August 4th 2006 the heart stopped of this remarkably wonderful human being citizen of Great Britain and our compatriot EKATERINA ALEXANDROVA TECLIK. In her 87 years she had lived through many events and diligently worked for the welfare of people.

She was a person bright, gifted, talented and of deep conviction. A person of action, good, generous and sympathetic.

Finding herself in Great Britain she maintained lively ties with the Ukraine and aspired to bring what was in her power her own unique contribution to the cultural unity of the twin towns of Barnsley and Gorlovka to the advantage of the people of England and the Ukraine.

The Town Council Executive Committee personally deeply mourn the end of a citizen of Great Britain our fellow countrywoman and great friend of the Ukraine.

TECLIK

EKATERINA ALEXANDROVA

And are expressing our sincere condolences to her family, relatives and near ones.

GLOSSARY

Astrakhan	Major city in South Russia that lies on the left bank of the Volga. The other being Archangel. Both cities were selected in 1941 in Operation Barbarossa to mark the eastern limits of German control.	P45
Chistakova – Chystyakova	Founded in 1778, a small settlement at confluence of river Sevostyanivka and Orlova by runaway serfs from different provinces of Ukraine and south of the Russian empire. 1964 Chystyakova was renamed Torez in honour of the French communist party leader Maurice Thorez in the year of his death.	P24
Donbas mining/ industrial region. Donetsk	Hughsovka named after a Welsh industrialist. 1924 renamed Stalino 1961 renamed Donetsk after Donets a tributary of the river Don.	P16
Dubas escape Carpathians - why?	Although politics and war has never had a simple explanation I will try and write a brief background to my understanding of different situations and points of view in the Ukraine amongst the populace. Poland – Carpathians 1918 After a century of partition of being ruled by Austro-Hungarian, German and Russian Empire Poland became independent.	P8

Dubas escape Carpathians - why (cont'd)	1917-19 Empire shattered, people of Ukraine caught in the middle. Different sections and armies, Bolshevik, Anarchist Freedom Army, Free German Army, Austrian, Ukrainian Peoples' Republic.	P8

1921 West Ukraine incorporated into
Poland. East Ukraine became part of Soviet
Union, Ukrainian Soviet Republic.

Forms of Foreign Labour	Once war began factories were nationalised. A class system was established for foreign workers who were brought to work for the Reich in Germany (about 12 million workers).	P65

Gastarbeitnehmer (Guest Worker)

Workers from neutral or allied countries,
Rumania, Bulgaria, Hungary and Italy. These
workers were paid well unlike slave workers
from conquered populations.

Ostarbeiter (Eastern Worker)

This is the category Katya and Misha (our
parents) were in.

Former Soviet civilian workers, mainly from
the Ukraine, marked with OST East. First
sent to intermediate camp where labour was
picked our directly by agents or companies.
Employed in agriculture, armaments, metal
production and railroads. Ostarbeiters had to
live in camps that were fenced with barbed
wire and under guard, exposed to the whims
of the Gestapo and industrial plant guards.

Forms of Foreign Labour (cont'd)	Ostarbeiters lived in both private camps owned and run by large companies and camps guarded by privately paid police known as Werkschutz.	P65

They worked on average 12 hours a day 6 days a week. They were paid about 30% less than the German workers wages. Most of the eastern workers money went towards their food, clothing and board. Many firms viewed them as "civilian prisoners" and paid no wages at all to the East workers.

Those who were paid were paid in specially printed money and saving stamps which could only be used to buy certain items in the camp stores. By law they were given worse food rations than other forced labour groups. Starvation rations and basic rough accommodation was given to these unfortunate people.

Ost workers were confined to their residence sometimes in labour camps and forbidden to associate with the Germans. The Germans considered Ukrainians as lesser humans who could be kicked, beaten, and frightened for the smallest offence. Many died when factories where they worked were bombed in allied raids. Many also died because German authorities ordered they should be worked to death.

| Forms of Foreign Labour (cont'd) | Nazi authorities tried to produce conditions on the farms where Ostarbeiters were integrated into their workforce while at the same time having social separation including not allowing them to eat at the same table as the other workers. As war worsened things improved as farmers tried to protect themselves against defeat. There were more female workers than male. | P65 |

Untermensch

Nazi term for people they considered sub human.

Zwangsarbeiter (Forced Labour)

Were individuals brought from Nazi occupied territories to work in German industries under harsh conditions.

Zivilarbietar (Civilian Workers)

Mainly Polish captives from the general government, regulated by strict Polish decrees. They got lower wages and couldn't use public conveniences.

| Italian POW | After Armistice between Italy and Allied forces on 8 September 8 1943 Italian soldiers and officers were given a choice, continue fighting in ranks of German army or be sent to POWs camps in Germany. Only 10% agreed to continue. An act in 1944 made them civil workers subject to hard labour without the protection of the Red Cross. | P129 |

NICKY	(mentioned in Foreword)
	Nicky was a boy with a sad childhood. At a young age his Italian Mother left his Ukrainian father taking her daughter (Nicky's sister) with her and leaving him aged 5 with his father.
	Though Nicky's father loved him he found it difficult working and looking after such a small child at the same time.
	Mama on hearing this from the Ukrainian community made the decision to unofficially become his surrogate mother and bring him home to Darfield from Doncaster to join her four children who were still at home.
	Later she officially fostered him. He became our Nicky and still is.

Nobel Alfred	Dynamite factory founded by Alfred Nobel & Co 1865. After the lst WW, parts of the factory were dismantled and forbidden to manufacture defence equipment after N Socials took lead in government they wanted to develop a strong defence industry. Factories were built on government land. During WW2 more than 100,000 people coming from camps managed by the ss were forced to work in more than 30 factories.	P128

POW	3,000 Jewish families were murdered by the Germans at (Stalino) Donetsk in WW2.	P59
	250,000 POWs buried in a mass grave who died in German POW camps in nearby (Stalino) Donetsk.	

Schmitz Hermann	German industrialist war criminal.	P71
Blechwaren-fabrik	Arrested by US army received 4 years in prison for crimes against humanity.	
World War 2	A large number of Ukrainians especially from the east (Donbas) were in the Red Army. The cruel actions of Soviet politics, eg famine in the wheat belt of Ukraine in 1933, massacre of intellectuals after the Polish annexe left a terrible fear and hate of Russians especially in Polish Ukraine.	P86

So when the German army approached, the West Ukrainians in the country side and villages saw them as liberators from the dreaded communists. Many of the Ukrainians joined the German ranks, some out of choice with other young men not given the option.